Reminisces of a Life in Ireland

1975 – 2015

Neil Williams

Introduction.

As I approach my 78th birthday, and as we are all locked-down due to the Covid19 pandemic, I feel that now would be a good opportunity to record some of my memories of the 40 years I lived and farmed in County Wexford, Ireland.

I am doing this purely for my own benefit whilst my mind is still sound (and hopefully will continue to be so – but you never know), and that perhaps there may be someone out there who might be interested in reading these observations.

After my dear wife, Anna died on 1st May 2014, I found it increasingly difficult living alone in a house that held so many memories. I therefore decided my best course would be to sell-up and move to England so that as I grow older, I will be nearer my siblings and their families. Apart from Anna's sister Liz Mellon and her partner Fi Read and a few friends such as Mitch and Tony Coote there is no one to keep me in Ireland. So, in April 2015 I sadly departed Ireland and moved to

England into an apartment I'd purchased in Scholars Court, Stratford-upon-Avon; a place that perfectly suites my needs. It is centrally located in the town and within easy walking distance of shops, doctors and pharmacies etc.

These are personal recollections and they may not concur with other people's memories of the same incidents. I have tried to be as accurate as possible with the events and people described herein, but it is entirely possible that I may have made some errors. After all they cover a long period of time and my memory is not perfect. Also, some of the happenings may seem trivial and irrelevant but I would like to record them anyway for my own benefit.

These notes are not in any chronological order but have been grouped into categories under different headings.

In the beginning…

I was born on the 25th April 1943 (which was Easter Sunday in that year) in the Warwickshire village of Bidford-on-Avon. The war in Europe was still ongoing and it would be two more years before Hitler's armies were finally defeated. I have a clear memory of two of my uncles coming home after being de-mobbed when the fighting was over. One had served in the Royal Navy on HMS Tenacious and the other as a soldier in North Africa.

I had a normal childhood growing up with my siblings in the rural countryside. I attended the local village infant and junior schools, before moving to the County High School and leaving at age 16 years, which was the norm at the time, and enlisting in the Royal Navy. (All these schools have subsequently disappeared, having been demolished to make way for housing). During these years as a family, we suffered the usual deprivations of shortages and rationing prevalent at the time. Rationing didn't end completely until 1954.

I first met Anna Mellon when she was working behind the bar of the Swans Nest Hotel in

Stratford-upon-Avon. I was living nearby at the time so this pub was my local and I'd regularly call in for a pint in the evenings. I struck up a conversation with her and it soon became clear that she didn't really know how to pull a pint of beer property. I gave her some pointers and tips on the correct method. It transpired that this was her first time working in a bar; she later admitted that she'd rarely entered a public house. Several evenings later I asked her if she'd like to go out on her next day off. She agreed, so we set off early in the morning and drove to Blackpool where we spent the day enjoying the rides at the pleasure beach. At that time, I owned a MGB convertible sports car which definitely impressed her.

Little did I realize at that time that this was the woman I was fated to share my life with, until her untimely death some 40 odd years later.

Anna and her sister Elizabeth had come to Stratford in the summer of 1972 to gain work experience in the hotel trade. Liz was put to work as a chamber maid and Anna was given the job of running the bar in the hotel. (A somewhat ambitious assignment considering her lack of experience).

The following year Anna graduated from Trinity College in Dublin and started a job as a trainee personnel manager in the Cumberland Hotel, at Marble Arch in London. She shared a flat in Warwick Avenue, Maida Vale, with Mary Kane, a childhood friend, and Margo Fermor. Mary was a solicitor and Margo was a Nursing Sister. Most weekends Anna would take the train from Paddington Station in London to Leamington Spa on a Friday evening where I'd meet her and she'd then return on Sunday. If I happened to be working in London, which I was on a several occasions doing demolition work for Birds, then I'd visit her.

At around this time, I moved from my flat in Tiddington Road, in Stratford to a farm cottage I rented in Snitterfield which belonged to Luscombe Farm. I shared it with my half-brother Richard (Dick) Hall. Although a small house it was still bigger than my previous flat. It was located nearer to Warwick than to Stratford.

Having served 12 years in the Royal Navy as a telecom's operator, and then worked for Bird's Commercial Motors, Long Marston for 5 years as a travelling site manager doing demolition work, I was beginning to feel it was time I settled down.

I'd been courting Anna for a couple of years by now and so I took the plunge and proposed to her one Saturday over lunch in the Rose and Crown pub (not very romantic, I know) in Warwick and she accepted.

I was invited to stay with Anna's family at 'Fey Yerra', their home in Foxrock, a suburb of Dublin, for Christmas 1973. We had decided that I would ask Anna's father for his permission (an old-fashioned idea) to marry his daughter when the opportunity presented itself on Christmas Day.

Anna's father, Leslie Mellon was a solicitor; the senior partner in the Dublin law firm of Orpen-Franks. Her mother Margaret (or Peggy as she was universally known) had trained at St Winifred's School in Llanfairfechan, near Conwy, North Wales as a children's nanny. The school had been established for the daughters of clergymen and professional men of limited means. Her father was the Reverent Dennis Rennison the rector of the parish of Tullamore, the county town of Offaly. Peggy's training as a children's nurse saw her employed by a doctor's family who lived for some time in Istanbul,

Turkey. Peggy accompanied them to look after their children.

On Christmas morning all the family attended Morning Prayer at St Bridget's Church in Stillorgan and afterwards returned to 'Fey Yerra'. It was a Mellon tradition that friends would call in for drinks after church on Christmas morning and before the Christmas meal was served at around 3 o'clock. These visitors included Leslie's brother Bill Mellon and his wife Sybil, the Rev Marcus Taylor his wife Trish and their sons, Simon and Maurice. Mr. Tom Gifford (I never learned what he did), and others I don't recall. Leslie always made a huge performance of mixing his 'famous' cocktail and serving it. I never discovered the recipe but it was very powerful, mostly gin I suspect.

Whilst we enjoyed the drinks Mrs Mellon divided her time between entertaining the guests and checking on Mrs O'Brien who was in the kitchen preparing the traditional meal of turkey and ham with all the trimmings. By one o'clock the cocktail drinkers had left and the dinner guests were arriving.

Seated for the meal on that Christmas day along with Mr. and Mrs Mellon, Anna, Liz and myself, were Peggy's sister Maureen Drennen and her two sons Neil and Anthony. (Peggy always referred to them as 'the boys'). Mr John Drennen (no relation), a soft-spoken, dapper man who always wore a rose bud in his buttonhole. Joan Plewes the next-door neighbour to the Mellon's and Dorothy Gore-Hickman, a frail looking woman who must have been well into her seventies. She was a redoubtable horse woman who hunted to hounds twice a week during the winter and exercised horses every day during the summer. With Mrs O'Brien there were 12 diners.

Mrs O'Brien (her name was Betty, but was always referred to as 'Mrs O'Brien') had been a long-time servant/cleaner to the Mellon's, but she never ate with the family as she didn't consider it her place to do so, so she ate alone in the kitchen, a hangover from the Victorian era where servants didn't mix socially with their masters. Paddy Bannan, who was the Mellon's gardener also ate with Mrs O'Brien in the kitchen whenever he was there working.

My plan was to ask Leslie if I could marry Anna during the postprandial walk but I was thwarted in this by the presence of Neil and Anthony Drennen who decided to accompany us. I didn't get another chance until the next day, St Stephen's Day or Boxing Day. Early the next morning Leslie, Peggy, Anna, Liz and I plus two dogs; Nubbin and Hazel bundled into Leslie's Rover P5B and drove the 90 odd miles to Garryduff, in Co Wexford and here I did get the chance to ask. Happily, approval was granted.

We were married in St Bridget's Church, Stillorgan on 29th June 1974. The ceremony was conducted by Anna's great uncle Eric Rennison, a long-retired cleric whom I know little about and who passed away soon after officiating.

My mother, Norah and her second husband, Len Hall; my brother Gary and his wife Noreen Williams; my sister Jane and her husband Keith Edkins; Glyn, and Julia, another brother and sister, all came over from England. They lodged in B&Bs in Dun Laoghaire.

Keith Edkins was my best man and Liz and Julia were Anna's bridesmaids. The reception was held at 'Fey Yerra' in a marquee that had been erected on the lawn. It was a beautiful hot sunny day and everyone except Anna and I got drunk. Finally, the ordeal of the ceremony and speeches were over and we were mercifully able to escape to Dublin airport and take a flight to Birmingham to start our honeymoon. At that time cheap package holidays abroad were unheard of and anyway we couldn't have afforded one so we spend a very enjoyable week driving around the Lake District and the Yorkshire Moors staying in hotels, pubs and B&B's.

Anna's father had recently sold 'Sweet Farm' a property he owned near Enniscorthy and had reinvested the proceeds into buying Garryduff, a much larger farm. At some time after we were married, we paid a weekend visit to Dublin where Leslie proposed that if I was willing to move to Ireland and work on the farm, we could live rent free in the house and I would receive a third of the profits on top of a salary.

At this time Anna had left her job in London and was working as a wages clerk for The British Pregnancy Advisory Service at Austy Manor, an establishment near Henley-in-Arden and she hated the job. By now I'd also become dissatisfied with my job at Bird's which required me to work away from the cottage in Snitterfield, only getting home at weekends. The job entailed an awful lot of driving in the little Morris 1000 van that Bird's provided. At one period I was commuting daily from the Midlands to South Wales. I was exhausted. So, when Leslie's offer came along, we both eagerly accepted it.

At this point in time The Land Commission in Ireland were being unfriendly toward what were termed 'Gentleman Farmers'. For over a century the Land Commission was the body responsible for the re-distribution of farmland in Ireland and was only formally abolished in 1999, They did not approve of investors buying land and simply sitting on it hoping that land prices would increase and a quick profit could be made with little or no input. A regulation was sanctioned that if land wasn't farmed properly the owners risked it being confiscated. So, by having me living and working there Leslie was officially able to state that it was a business and a working farm; an arrangement that suited all parties.

Life in Ireland

And so began my life in Ireland. We arrived from England on 5th January 1975 and twenty years later in the summer of 1995 we left Garryduff when the farm was sold. During this twenty-year period James and Cass were born.

James Leslie was born on 10th August 1977 and Cassandra Margaret on 7th February 1979. Both children were delivered in the Rotunda Hospital in Dublin. Anna endured an agonising 12 hours of labour giving birth to James; Cass's delivery on the other hand was much easier and quicker. (Like shelling peas). As the date of Cass's birth approached, we were starting to become quite anxious. That February was very cold, with heavy frosts and a lot of snow and ice, we were worried that we wouldn't make it to Dublin on time. But it all turned out well and Cass was born after only a short labour.

James Leslie was named after my grandfather, James Teale and Leslie after Anna's father. Cassandra was a name we both liked and Margaret after Anna's mother.

Both children were educated in Ireland. To begin with they attended a small single teacher school at Kilnamanagh. Before they were born, we gave a commitment to Rev Robert Stewart, the parish rector, that we would send the children to this school so that there would be sufficient numbers for it to remain open. This turned out to be a mistake, although at the time we didn't know it. There was a total of 27 kids in the school ranging from Junior Infants to year 6 all being taught by the one teacher, Loraine Rössler. She tried her best but I think she was simply overwhelmed by the numbers. There were 4 pupils in James' year and the same in Cass's and it soon became evident that they were not learning anything. Further to this James was very unhappy and we later learned he was being bullied by Loraine who would shout at him, pull his hair and banish him to the bathroom.

We moved James first and enrolled him in St. Mary's School in Enniscorthy with Cass following a year later. St. Mary's had about 90 students on the roll overseen by Mrs Farrah, the formidable headmistress. She was assisted by Mrs Tomkins and Ms Wilkinson. Both children thrived under this regime. It was here that James met his life-long friend Noel Warren. On graduation from St Mary's James and Noel moved to the Vocational College or the 'Tech' in Bunclody where he did well, excelling in practical skills. Unfortunately, during his final year he and Noel were involved in an incident with several other youths which involved damage to one of the teachers' cars. The upshot was he was obliged to move schools to the Christian Brothers school in Enniscorthy which he hated. He began truanting and finally opted out altogether. As he had completed his obligatory educational schooling this wasn't too serious, but he was spending his days moping around the house doing nothing. I finally issued an ultimatum; either he continues his schooling or he gets himself a job. To his credit he very soon found employment assisting Brian McGann, an émigré from Scotland, in building his house. He was later employed by Paddy Jennings (about more later) in the building trade where he served his apprentaship.

When Cass left St Mary's she continued her schooling at Newtown School in Waterford as a boarder. Newtown is a Quaker run school and produced a large number of university entrants. Cass gained a place in University College Galway, where she attained a BA International degree. To qualify for this, she won an Erasmus Mundus Scholarship which involved spending a year as an exchange student studying in the University of Granada in Spain where she became fluent in Spanish and studied Spanish history. Anna and I visited her in Granada and holidayed in Cadiz with her and a group of her friends. Afterwards we travelled to Seville to see the Seville Fare and then on to Madrid by high-speed train where we took in the Prado Museum and did the usual site seeing tours. Whilst at the Prado Anna's handbag was grabbed by a youth who ran off with it. Fearing its loss along with her passport and credit cards and the usual assortment of items contained within she was very surprised when a plain-clothes policeman returned it to her. Several detectives had been surreptitiously watching the crowds when he saw the theft and arrested the villain.

Later in life both children emigrated; James to Canada and Cass to Chile. Both of them married; James to Khudeja Rehmanji, where they lived in Vancouver before later moving to London, Ontario. Cass married Eugenio (Queno) Medina and they lived in various suburbs of Santiago. I now have seven grandchildren – Two by James - Adam and Ali and five of Cass's - Benjamin,

Matteo, and the triplets - Emilio, Amalia and Anna.

Farming

During that first couple of months at Garryduff I seriously began to think that I'd made a major mistake in moving to Ireland. It rained constantly throughout January and February; I was always wet and cold. The house was undergoing major renovations at the time restricting us to the kitchen and one bedroom only. There was very little comfort or warmth. But with the coming of spring things improved and I began to enjoy the work.

I began to learn the mysteries and intricacies of farming, although having been born and reared in the English countryside I had a basic knowledge of agriculture. Dan Furlong (about more later) was supposed to mentor me, but it soon became apparent that he was quite hopeless at explaining and describing the procedures and practices of farming. Apart from the difficulty of understanding what he said, he was quite inarticulate. For instruction I regularly attended the Teagasc Centre (The Irish Agriculture and Food Development Authority) in Enniscorthy for lectures and demonstrations on the latest farming techniques. I also read widely and watched what other farmers were doing. Dan didn't approve of modern farming ideas preferring the old ways of doing things which resulted in many disagreements. In that first year I also learned a lot about animal husbandry and the health and welfare of stock keeping.

When I began working at Garryduff, we had about 30 head of cattle – all bullocks or steers, mostly Herefords with a few Charolais, which were over-wintered in the fields. To keep them fed required the loading of a trailer with hay and driving it out to the field twice a day. Over the following few years, the cattle numbers were gradually increased to over a hundred head, which were wintered in sheds and yards which we'd built or converted. During the winter month the feeding and cleaning out of the sheds was more or less a full-time job; seven days a week.

Many years later we switched from producing bullocks to heifers as they were making a better price. The supermarkets preferred the meat. We also embarked on a calf rearing enterprise. Calves were purchased at weaning age and were reared to yearlings. They were prone to diseases particularly pneumonia of which several succumbed and were lost. Another affliction prevalent in them was ringworm. It would often cross to humans but was easily treated with creams. When my mother and sister Julia visited one summer, Julia became a victim and took the infection back to England with her.

This number of animals naturally required a vast amount of hay (one year we made 11,000 bales) and summers were spent mowing, baling and hauling the bales into the sheds; a back-breaking and tiring procedure. At the busiest times when we were drawing in the hay bales, our neighbours the Hawkins' would sometimes lend a hand. Later on, we employed Gerald Dempsey (who lived in Boolavogue) to assist Dan and myself. By this time, we had acquired newer bale handling machinery and the need to load trailers with pitch forks in the fields then unload them again into the sheds was no longer necessary. As the years progressed, we used the newest machines that processed the hay into large round bales which required even less labour.

In one of the earlier years Leslie thought it would be a great idea to arranged for half a dozen students to help us with the haymaking. This didn't work out too well though, as that summer turned out to be very wet and the students spent most of their time sitting around all day eating us out of house and home.

Our principal farming activities were rearing beef cattle and the growing of cereal crops. Garryduff had fifteen fields of various acreages and all had names. Some were obvious, such as the Lawn Field; which was often the name given to the field in front of the farm house; the Lime Kiln Field in which years ago there'd been an incinerator where lime was burned to use as fertilizer, and the Five Corner Field because of its shape. Others were more obscure; the Bullock Field, the Brow Field and the Paling Field among others, whose names had survived over the years but whose origins had been lost.

The autumn was the time for ploughing after the harvest was over and done with. Dan always liked to have all the ploughing done before Christmas so that the winter weather would help to break down the soil. Then in the Spring, as soon as the land was workable the tilling would begin. First harrowing to obtain a fine seed bed, before drilling the barley, wheat or oat seed. When that was all done, there followed the worst job of the year – picking stones. Every year a huge number of rocks and stones would be collected from the newly sown fields. The quantity never seemed to get any less. I optimistically expected that the following year there would not be any left to pick up but there was always as many again. Where they all came from, I never figured out. But it was a sole-destroying, back breaking job that took days and days to do. It had to be done, of course because a rock picked up by a combine harvester or baler could do considerable damage to the machine.

All the land that wasn't needed for grazing or for hay was sown with cereals, wheat, barley or oats, grown in a strict rotation. Most of the barley was stored in a barn and used during the winter months to feed the cattle. Any surplus was sold to Kevin Cooney Ltd at Raheenduff as well as the wheat. The oats were sold to Frank Dunne a horse trainer to feed his race-horses. Some years later we purchased grain silos in which we were able to store the wheat and barley, so getting a better price for it later in the year.

Straw from the cereals was baled and used as bedding for the cattle during the winter months. At that time, it was customary for the surplus straw to be burned in the fields. (The practice has since been stopped). This was fine during calm weather, but I remember one occasion when having put a match to the straw the wind suddenly picked up and the fire raced across the ground at an alarming speed. I was totally helpless to stop it. Before I knew it the flames were licking up against Victor Hawkins' garage, melting his plastic windows and jumping over the hedge into Eddie Guests barley. I was powerless to halt it and was definitely beginning to panic. Then, out of nowhere, it seemed, who should appear but Martin Donohoe with his tractor and plough.

Martin was the son of John Donohoe, a neighbour, who happened to be passing and immediately saw and understood my predicament. He quickly ploughed a fire-break around the perimeter of the field and we were able to extinguish the fire and so avoid a total calamity. I often wonder what would have happened had not Martin appeared when he did.

With so much grain and fodder stored in the barns, rats were a major problem. No matter what

I tried I could never get on top of them. I purchased poison by the 5-kilo bucket full and laid it down the holes and on their well-defined runs, but still they continued to flourish. A trick we employed was to suddenly open the door to the barn where the barley was stored and let Monty (Dan's dog) in. He was usually able to catch four or five before they disappeared. Later Nellie turned out to be an excellent ratter too. It was a miracle that neither Dan nor I contracted Weils Disease with so much rat urine everywhere.

Entertainment

Those first few years were a struggle for us as we never seemed to have enough money; we couldn't afford holidays, to go out much, or give ourselves treats. In those early years we had no television, (there was only one black and white channel anyway), so we'd spend our evenings reading or playing cribbage. Sometimes I'd read aloud while Anna knitted or crocheted.

When colour television was still a novelty and it cost a huge amount of money to buy a set, the normal practice was to rent one. With the coming of the 1980 Moscow Olympic Games, we decided that we should go ahead and hire one. I went along to Astor TV Rentals in Enniscorthy and arranged with Keith Doyle to rent a set. (It was an enormous wooden box) I can't remember how much the weekly payments were but we often found that we couldn't afford them. When Astor sent a man round to collect it, I'm ashamed to say that I would sometimes hide so as to put off having to pay.

In the summer of the following year, Anna luckily managed to get a job as a nursery school assistant in Enniscorthy which helped with the finances. At around this time she also undertook surveys for Lansdowne Market Research a Dublin firm of market pollsters and canvassers. Unfortunately, these jobs involved an awful lot of driving to collect the data and the cost of petrol more or less equalled what she earned so it was not very lucrative.

In the nursery school she worked with Susan Mosse with whom she became great friends, and it was through Sue that Anna met other young women. They met each week at one another's houses for a 'sewing bee' and gradually she expanded her circle of friends. Our social life improved over time too and we eventually got to know a wide group of people all of similar ages to us and were regularly invited for drinks or dinner parties.

On one such occasion we were invited to Rory and Angela Dunne's house in Macmine for a drinks party. It was not long after James had been born and not being able to get a baby sitter, we bundled him up in his Moses basket, put it into the back of our Renault 4L and drove to the party. We parked the car at the front of the house and left James sleeping in the back checking on him regularly of course. (Social Services would definitely not have approved). At the end of the evening Anna insisted on driving home as she claimed she was less drunk that I was. However, driving along the narrow lanes in the area she misjudged the distance to the side of the road and put the car into a ditch. There was no hope of getting it out so I said I'd walk home and get a tractor to tow it out. I quickly realized how ridiculous that idea was as it was a moonless black night and not having any sort of torch I couldn't see where I was going. (I always kept a flash light in the car after that). Luckily a neighbour came along a gave us a lift home. He was shocked to see that we had a baby in a basket out at night, but throughout the entire evening

James never once woke up. The next morning Dan and I took a tractor and pulled the car out of the ditch. Fortunately, it was undamaged apart from a few dents and scratches. Those were the days, of course before there were any laws prohibiting drinking and driving and we were still a bit irresponsible.

When we'd been living at Garryduff for some years, a tradition started of holding a party on New Year's Eve. We invited friends from all over the country; from Dublin, Gorey, Enniscorthy, Wexford and even from England to attend. Anna would make a big pot of curry or stew from which people helped themselves and the guests would bring bottles of booze. As we grew older and became more sedate, we'd sit everyone in the dining room for a formal meal. The most we managed to entertain in a single sitting was 14, which was no mean feat considering our limited resources.

As midnight approached every one trooped out to the yard, (I don't remember the weather ever being inclement; it was often cold and frosty) and the bell that hung atop the stables was rung. I would ring it sixteen times following a Navy custom of ringing eight bells for the old year and eight for the new. After a few years the local people would listen out for the ringing. On still frosty nights the bell could be heard for many miles around.

A bell was a common feature on farms in the pre-tractor era. It was rung to summon the workers in from the fields for their dinner and it was said that if the men didn't hear it then the horses would. Quite how Garryduff's bell survived is a bit of a mystery as most were removed to be melted down during the war.

Some of the people who attended the parties over the years included; Jonathon and Susan Bailey, Anthony and Jennifer Aston, Steven Booth, Pat and Liz Faulkner, Justin McCarthy, Michael and Maria Warren, Richard and Cathy Warren, Jonathon Peel, Jossey Proby, Mike and Cathy Marshall and others I've forgotten.

On one memorable New Year's party Jossey Proby (a childhood friend of Anna's) attended together with her new boyfriend. (His name was Bill something-or-other). A slight young man who was nervous and shy never having experienced an Irish party. He worked as a stockbroker or a banker in London and was totally bemused by the boisterous gathering of intoxicated people gathered in Garryduff. In sharp contrast to Bill was Steven Booth. He was a huge man (six foot five and at least 20 stone) and a formidable drinker. He played hooker for Old Wesley Rugby Club and was quite fearsome on the rugby field. Steve arrived late and was well lubricated by the time he turned up having stopped at almost every pub between Dublin and Wexford. He was in expansive form and during the course of the evening Steve took it upon himself to regale Jossey's boyfriend with stories of his adventures on the rugby field. However, maintaining his balance after so much drink eventually proved too much for Steven who in a vain attempt to remain upright seized Bill in a bear hug, and slowly collapsed to the floor taking Bill with him, pinning the poor chap to the floor under his considerable weight. After the startled man was extricated, Steven spent the remainder of the night lying where he'd fallen in the middle of the drawing room floor. Everyone simply stepped over or around him. He remembered very little the following morning only that it was a great party.

When the party finally broke up at two or three o'clock in the morning, the revellers jumped into their cars and roared off. There was lots of shouting, blowing of horns and revving engines. Amazingly everyone got home safely; again, this was before the drink driving laws were enacted.

As a post-script, Steven sadly died a couple of years after this from an aggressive form of lung cancer.

Ghosts

There were persistent tales and anecdotes that Garryduff was haunted. They had prevailed for many years and from long before we came to live there. Some stories even dated back to the 1798 rebellion when the house was used to garrison British troops before the battle of Oulart Hill. At one time Jane Stewart (a cousin of Anna's) stayed overnight and at breakfast the following morning she asked who had been frying bacon rashers and talking loudly during the night. It was not possible we answered because (a) there was no bacon in the house at the time and (b) everybody was asleep in bed. On another occasion a guest complained about the noise made by squealing pigs; again, it wasn't possible because at that time there were no pigs on the farm. People said they often heard clocks striking when there were no clocks in the room and at one time Anna swore, she saw a small girl in a white nightdress standing at the top of the stairs. (This was before Cass was born). Dan Furlong was convinced that a coach and four could often be heard driving down the lane on certain nights. If there were any ghosts, they were benign and friendly and certainly not scary. I spent many nights alone in the house when Anna was away in Dublin and only on one occasion did, I ever experience anything vaguely supernatural; I thought I heard someone walking around upstairs but on investigating I found nothing; it was probably mice. James and Cass never heard or saw anything untoward. I suspect these stories may have contributed to the house being abandoned after we left; neither the Bailey's who had bought the farm nor anyone else wanted to live in it.

Visitors

Anna's Mum and Dad came to Garryduff every weekend without fail. They arrived on Saturday lunchtime with their dogs and stayed until Sunday evening. Accompanying them was always 'the box'. It was a battered old cardboard box (which was never exchanged for a new one), in which Peggy brought any left-overs they happened to have from previous meals as well as Leslie's bottle of Brandy and any half-finished bottles of wine. For some reason this thing used to irritate me enormously. It was partly the fact that Peggy assumed that we wanted her left-overs and partly the presumption that we were so hard up we couldn't afford to buy them ourselves. To be fair, her intentions were good I suppose.

The only exception to their weekend visits was when they took their annual two-week fishing holiday to Newport House Hotel in Co Mayo. Their constant presence at Garryduff was at times very annoying as it meant that as a family we couldn't go anywhere on weekends or bank holidays as Anna was expected to be at home to cook meals and entertain them. It became a source of friction between Leslie and I, and poor Anna was left to conciliate.

They always brought along their three dogs; Nubbin and Hazel, which were Springer Spaniels and Martha, an Old English Sheepdog who actually belonged to Liz. Later after Nubbin and Hazel had died, they were replaced by Louise another Springer and Ivory, a Black Labrador.

(An ironic name). Along with our dogs there could well be five or six dogs altogether in the kitchen at any one time, and it could get very noisy especially when the occasional fight broke out. Nubbin was an untrustworthy dog with a killer instinct. On one occasion when they arrived, Leslie opened the car door and Nubbin jumped out and made straight for the duck pond. Before he could be stopped, he had massacred 8 or 10 ducks. Those he didn't kill outright had to be finished off. Such wanton destruction was very upsetting, but I suppose you couldn't blame the dog, it was his natural impulse.

Holidays

As the children grew older, we insisting on taking two weeks holiday each year. We usually rented a self-catering cottage in Ireland. Over the years we holidayed at Timoleague, Reenascreena, Trabolgan, Ballylikey and several time we rented John O'Shea's house overlooking the bay at Glengarriff in County Cork.

These Glengarriff holidays were the best because on a couple of occasions Mike Marshall (an old friend of mine) joined us with his two boys,

Anthony and David. They were a bit older than James and Cass but were great friends. This was the time soon after Mike and Jane Marshall had divorced and Mike was glad of any excuse to get away from where he lived. He also came and stayed at Garryduff with his lads and he occasionally turned up for the New Year's parties.

On most days if the sun was shining, (and it often seemed that it did) we'd load up the car and drive the 10 miles to Zetland Pier and spend the day swimming and sun bathing at the rock pool; a natural cove in Bantry Bay. It was here that Mike, who was staring through a pair of binoculars claimed to have spotted an Albatross much to our hilarity.

There was a small island just off the shore at Zetland harbour with a holiday house owned by Sir Bernard Lovell (he of the Jodrell Bank telescope fame) which was used by his relatives for holidays. One family's visits coincided with ours and James and Cass became friendly with their kids. We called them the 'A's' because they were named Alice, Andrew and Annabelle. They would row a small boat over from the island to the pier and spend the day at the rock pool with us.

If the weather was inclement, we'd go to Killarney or Kenmare or drive to the Beara Peninsular or the Ring of Kerry or some other interesting place. Once or twice, we took a ferry boat over to Garnish Island which the kids loved. There were any number of intimidating and bullying boatmen who competed with each other for your custom. Sometimes they almost came to blows with each other to secure a fare.

Garnish is a small island in the middle of Glengarriff Bay. It's famous for its tropical plants, Martello Tower and Italianate Garden.

On one of our Rent-a-Cottage holidays, we stayed in a house near Timmoleague, Co Cork. Cass (who was about 3 or 4 years old at the time) suffered a series of unfortunate accidents all on the same day. As we were about to leave for a picnic at the beach, Cass, who'd been repeatably told to hurry up fell down the stairs in her haste. She cart-wheeled down landing in a heap at the bottom. I think she was too shocked and surprised to cry and apart from a few bruises she was unhurt. Later in the day she announced that a bumble bee had bitten her. And sure, enough Anna found a sting on her arm. The third disaster to befall the child happened when we were strolling along the beach at Owenahincha near Glandore. Looking in a rock pool she spotted a dolls leg lying on the bottom of one pool. Not realizing how deep the water was she reached in for it but her arms were not long enough to reach the bottom and she topple in head first. Luckily, I was close by and saw what was happening and I grabbed her by the ankle and pulled her up. Cass was shocked and upset but otherwise okay. She could easily have drowned had no one seen her fall. She carried that dolls leg everywhere for the remainder of the holiday.

Another popular excursion for a day out was to Clara Lara Adventure Park in Co. Wicklow. It had originally been a trout farm that had gone bust and so the owner (I can't remember his name) decided to turn it into a recreation ground, utilising the defunct fish ponds and streams. It was mostly rope swings over the rivers, wobblily rope bridges and a few boats on the lake. Nothing too elaborate. I got great entertainment from watching the dad's showing their children how to swing across a stream. "Stand aside, son, this is how you do it". Trouble was they no longer had the upper body strength they once had nor were as strong as they were as teenagers. They inevitably fell in. The Park was later closed down by Health and Safety because the owner was operating without insurance.

Work

Our living standard dramatically improved when Anna successfully applied for a job as a social worker with NCBI (National Council for the Blind of Ireland). As a regional manager she was responsible for about a hundred and fifty clients in the south-east of the country. The job came with a car (a Citroën AX) and a tiny office in the Athenaeum (a meeting hall cum theatre) in Enniscorthy. The 'office' also housed all the electrical switch boards for the theatre as well as it being a store room for cleaning supplies. When Father Martin Kenny, a catholic priest who did voluntary work for the organization saw it, he was appalled and quickly found Anna a new home for her office in Henrietta Street in Wexford town. Father Kenny was in the process of setting up a thrift shop in Wexford at the time and there was space in the building for an office.

Father Kenny went on to establish a chain of charity shops across Ireland named 'Mrs Quinn's'. He'd established about forty-five shops across the country before his untimely death in his early forties. Before his death he had left the priesthood and married a woman he had known since childhood.

After Anna had been with NCBI for a few years she persuaded the members of Wexford Urban and District Councils to purchase the derelict cinema building in Harpers Lane and with grants from various bodies, including the National Lottery converted it into a social facility named 'Lochrann Centre.' As well as NCBI, the Irish Wheelchair Association and the Wexford Deaf Association also had offices in the building. The centre was primarily used for teaching visually impaired patron's life and cooking skills. They also provided the members with a hot meal. Among the many projects they undertook was the formation of a choir and the recording of a compact disc. Under the supervision of Michael Benson, a social worker for NCBI, a group of clients built and launched a rowing boat onto the Slaney River. The whole venture proved to be a great success. The centre was officially opened by the President of Ireland Mrs Mary McAleese. Mr

Des Kenny CEO of NCBI, the Mayor of Wexford and other local dignities also attended. Anna continued to be employed by NCBI right up until her death.

Life after farming.

With the sale of Garryduff I effectively became redundant. We moved to a new house with a small-holding of some 20 acres named Tristenagh, in Glenbrien. As there was not enough land to make farming practicable, I had to find employment elsewhere. I considered using my farming experience to do relief work but this mostly consisted of milking other farmers cows, and as I had no experience of this work, I rejected it as a possible source of employment.

An acquaintance had asked me if I would be willing to drive a school bus, but as I didn't have the requisite licence, I had to decline. I mentioned this to Mr Mellon who offered to finance me to train for the PSV driving test in Dublin. Once having passed the test and obtained my 'D' licence, Joe Murray offered me a job. Joe operated three buses and one of his drivers had recently quit so I luckily started right away. I collected school children from the Enniscorthy area and brought them to the Vocational college and the FCJ (Faithful Companions of Jesus) schools in Bunclody. I also did the occasional trips to Bingo nights and a few weddings. I did this for a couple of years until Joe unfortunately had a stroke and was forced to sell the business.

Luckily for me Brendan Edwards, another bus operator in the area bought his assets and employed me along with them. Now as a change from school runs, I collected 6 or 7 severely disabled young adults, and delivered them to St Patricks Special School in Enniscorthy. These young people could be unpredictable and volatile. I remember one occasion, as I was nearing the school one of the clients suddenly went berserk. He was a large young man named Ivan. For no apparent reason he suddenly picked on one of the girls. He tore the coat off her back and ripped it to pieces, terrifying the poor girl and leaving her in tears. He then ripped up the seat from the floor of the minibus, a feat requiring considerable strength, and threw it at the rear window of the bus smashing it. I had to do an emergency stop, to retrieve the seat and admonish Ivan who I eventually calmed down. I reported his behaviour to Mrs Leach, the school principal of St Patricks, and Ivan was sent home. He wasn't allowed back to the school and I never saw him again. I did this work for about three years until Brendan lost the contract and I was again unemployed.

Fortuitously, Ard Aobhann Centre, were looking for a driver at this time, the previous driver had become ill and been forced to give up work. Ard Aobhann is a centre for people with special needs in Wexford town. I applied for and was offered the job as their second driver. My experience with the patrons attending St Patricks School was a great help in securing me the position as well as holding the correct licence to drive a bus. The work required me to pick up clients from around the county, secure their wheelchairs in the bus and bring them into the centre, then return them home in the evenings. They ranged in age from pre-teens to late twenties and their infirmities comprised mild Downs syndrome to severe mental and physical incapacities. I enjoyed the work and continued doing it until I was obliged to retire at age 65.

Garryduff and Neighbourhood

Garryduff lies in the Civil Parish of Kilcormick, the Electoral District of Kilcormick and the Barony of Ballaghkeen North in the county of Wexford.

The townland of Garryduff is situated approximately 5 miles from Enniscorthy which is the largest nearby town; it is 2 miles from the villages of Boolavogue and the same distance from Monogear. The county town of Wexford is 15 miles away and Dublin the capital is 90 odd miles.

Townlands bordering Garryduff are Garrybrit Upper and Garrybrit Lower, Kilcormick, Clondaw, Grange, Ballincash Upper and Ballincash Lower and Kilconib.

In the 1800's Garryduff and the adjoining townland of Grange were owned by Lady Henrietta Geary and was tenanted to William Goodison. At this time Garryduff had a total area of 321 acres and Grange totalled 322 acres giving a total of 643 acres. Over the following decades and during the famine years the Goodison family dispersed; some emigrating to Canada and the US

41

and others to Australia. Details are sketchy because of the absence of reliable records.

Following the Goodison's tenure the tenancy passed to Alexander Roberts. The 1911 census lists Roberts living there with his wife Ellen, there two daughters, Michael Elizabeth and Mary Alexandra along with two servants. The Roberts were a Quaker family.

At some date during the following years the Roberts' left and the Black family became the residents; they were followed by Henry Binnions and his family, and in 1973 Garryduff was bought by Leslie Mellon. In 1995 the property again changed hands being sold to Christopher Bailey who, so far as I know is still the owner.

Over the years from the time of the Goodisons, the land had been divided and parcels sold off until by the time Leslie Mellon bought it Garryduff was a mere 170 acres.

There was a large Protestant community living in the area and they attended the church of St Cormac at Kilcormac. When we arrived and first attended the Rector was Canon Robert Stewart. He was a likeable elderly man whose death in the

1980's left the parish without a priest. To avoid the closure of the church the parish was incorporated into the Ferns Union administered by the Dean of St Eden's Cathedral the Rev David Earl. Both Anna and Leslie were inducted as Lay Readers as part of the effort to save the church.

Supplies of seed and fertilizers were purchased from Kevin Cooney Ltd at their depot at Raheenduff. They were also the principal buyers of the cereals grown by us and most of the other farmers in the area. Other goods and spare parts were acquired from various places such as John Donohue Ltd, George Kehoe Ltd and the Enniscorthy Farmers Co-Op. Cattle, calves and sheep were bought and sold in the Enniscorthy Livestock Mart and occasionally from Gorey Mart.

Veterinary services were provided by Messrs Kavanagh and Kent in Enniscorthy. Simon Kavanagh was the senior vet and was semi-retired. He was a constant sufferer with Brucellosis contracted from dairy cattle years previously. Martin Kent specialized in horses and would attend us whenever a horse needed treatment or to confirm that the mares were in foal. He would also register new born foals. The community was greatly shocked when Martin unexpectedly dropped dead at Wexford races from a brain aneurysm. Other vets in the practice were Michael O'Shea and Larry Wall plus students getting practical experience. Before the opening of their new premises on the Dublin Road (every town and village in Ireland has a Dublin Road) they operated from premises in the yard at the rear of 'Buttles's Barley-Fed Bacon Factory'. An outfit where pigs were slaughtered and butchered. On killing days their squeals could be heard all over the town. The veterinary facilities were somewhat limited and it was not uncommon to see large animals such as calves and ewes being operated on in the open air. Whoever owned the animal would be expected to assist with the operation.

The Furlongs

Daniel and Josephine Furlong were both in their mid-fifties when I first met them. Dan had been employed at Sweetfarm; the farm Mr Mellon owned before he'd bought Garryduff. They had subsequently moved to Garryduff where Dan continued to work maintaining the farm and doing small jobs. To accommodate them Leslie built a small bungalow or gatelodge at the top of the lane adjacent to the entrance. Until this was completed, they had lived in the big house and had become accustomed to the status this conferred, so that when we arrived, they were reluctant to move and this caused a certain amount of resentment towards us.

Dan had worked alone and unsupervised for some years and he therefore thought of himself as the boss and could do pretty much what he wanted. It took him some time to accept my involvement and the changes that followed.

Dan had been one of nine children born in a small two-up, two-down council cottage at Clondaw. Apart from his brother Nicolas who lived nearby, and another brother Michael who occasionally visited from England I didn't know any of the

45

others. The house had no electricity or running water and the heating and cooking was done on a turf burning range. Dan's father worked as a farm hand and made shoes by candle light in the evenings.

The Furlongs had married late in life and had no children. Their courtship had lasted many years and by the time they had got around to marrying it was too late for them to start a family. Except for an excursion to the Isle of Mann, Dan had never travelled outside the country. Mrs Furlong came originally from Adamstown. I know very little about her family and background as she never spoke of it. Likewise, I don't know how they met. At some point in her life, she travelled to the Isle of Mann (the reasons for which I know not). Dan followed her and persuaded her to come back.

Dan was a big man; standing over six feet in height and heavily built. He possessed tremendous strength and was capable of carrying two 50 kilo bags of fertilizer with one under each arm.

It was several months before I fully understood what he was saying. He spoke with a heavy

Wexford accent and mumbled as though his mouth was full of bread. He used words and expressions that were alien to me. On one occasion, not long after our arrival he announced that he was - "going to slap a dart a lime on the piers". Having no idea what he was talking about I surreptitiously snook up on him and discovered that he was in fact painting the entry gates posts with white-wash.

He spoke of 'schiochs' which were blackthorn trees, (in fact the word could refer to almost any hedgerow bush); Willows were 'Sallies', (probably from the Latin Salix). Manure forks were 'sprongs', ants were 'pismires' and 'brus' or 'brussy' was straw used for bedding cattle and horses (I subsequently learned the word came from the Gaelic for litter). Anyone fooling around was 'alligating', and someone being cheeky or talking back was 'imperrent'. (a portmanteaux word from impudent and impertinent).

He used old fashioned expressions, for example he always referred to Anna as 'Mistress' and to Mr Mellon as 'Master'. He took things 'asunder' when he meant to dismantle it. Ill cattle inevitably had the 'murrain' irrespective of what was wrong with them and when they had diarrhoea they were scouring. And the colour brown was always red for some reason. Having been raised in a house with no indoor plumbing he was accustomed to going behind a hedge or a bank to do his business and would announce the he was going to "ease me self" whenever he needed to go. I finally had to forbid the practice after Florrie (see Dogs) rolled in the results of one such easement.

He could be awkward and cantankerous (usually after a night on the booze). I'd get infuriated whenever we disagreed on something or other regarding a farming operation; instead of offering an opinion or suggestion he'd sulk and mutter "I'm saying nothing" then obstinately refuse any further discussion.

Like most Irishmen he loved horses. He'd sometimes reminisced about when as a young lad he worked as a stable boy for Bill Black looking after the working horses. He was responsible for their grooming, feeding and the maintenance of the tack. He'd sometimes even sleep with them if one was not well. In the days before mechanization horses did all the work and it was important to keep them healthy. He reckoned it was a good day's work for a man to plough an acre of land. I've no idea how many miles a man would walk in a day following a pair of horses pulling a single furrow plough but it must have been many. He loved racing too. Whenever there was a race meeting in Wexford or Kilkenny or Goran Park, Dan would be gone for the day no matter what had to be done. He also had the same attitude when Holy Days came round, of which there seemed to be an awful lot.

Dan was very fond of the Guinness. Come Saturday lunchtime he'd dress in his Sunday best and off he'd go to Miley Kehoe's pub where he'd spend the day getting drunk. The same would happen after Mass on Sunday's. But he always remembered to buy a packet of chocolate biscuits for James and Cass that he'd pass through the kitchen window on Monday morning.

Before my arrival any errands to collect spare parts or whatever would be an excuse for Dan to disappear into town. He'd collect whatever it was then head for Miley's Bar. And that would be the last seen of him till the next morning. He was most put out when I ran the errands depriving him of a session.

A lifetime of drinking eventually took its toll on his health. He was several times hospitalized with bleeding ulcers and chest pains and ultimately underwent a triple heart by-pass operation. After that he was never the same man again and was eventually persuaded to retire. In lieu of a pension Leslie bought them a cottage in Kilconib where he and Josie lived for many years before moving into Enniscorthy where he died.

Mrs Furlong's name was Josephine or Josie as she was known to her friends. She was also called Dolly Furlong and on one occasion I heard her referred to as Dolly Taylor, but she was always Mrs Dan to us. I'm not sure how this came about but I believe it was because Leslie didn't want to use the formal title of Mrs Furlong nor did he want to be too personal and call her Josie, so Mrs Dan was the compromise.

In the beginning she was employed to clean the house as a means of supplementing Dan's wages. Her duties were originally to work two days a week but over time this had gradually reduced to working on Saturday mornings only. From hoovering, polishing and dusting all the rooms she finally ended up just washing the kitchen floor. She unfortunately suffered from mental problems and had been prescribed medication to treat it but I'm not sure she always took the pills, or took them as she was supposed to. She would spend long periods staring out of the kitchen window, scratching her head and muttering under her breath. It was most disconcerting to see.

Every afternoon she would drive off in her little Fiat Panda to visit someone or other where she would sit and expect to be given tea and cakes. She made no attempt at conversation and was content to simply sit and listen. Anna heard from several of the people whom she visited that they began to dread her visits as they couldn't do anything for themselves whilst she was there.

The Furlongs owned three dogs – Monty, who was Dan's cattle dog (a dislikeable creature) and Wendy and Cindy all Border Collies. Monty had never been properly trained to herd cattle or sheep and only half comprehended what Dan wanted him to do. Dan would shout unintelligibly and wave his arms like a demented scarecrow and expect the dog to understand what it was supposed to do. It inevitably resulted in the cattle stampeding instead of being quietly herded together. Monty drove Anna mad too. Every morning the dog would carefully deposit a pile of excrement on the gravel at the front of the house which had to be cleaned up.

Mrs Dan kept innumerable cats that without exception suffered from some form of illness. They inter-bred prolifically and Dan would regularly drown the latest litter of kittens in a water butt. He would occasionally drown mature cats too which I thought was horribly inhumane. They were nearly always unwell but she wouldn't take them to the Vets because it was (a) too expensive and (b) they were only cats. Anna and I offered to do it but she wouldn't allow it.

After Dan died Mrs Furlong lived for many years alone in the little cottage, they had bought on Island Road in Enniscorthy. She died in August 2015.

The Neighbours

The following are some of our immediate neighbours but not all. Even though we were at Garryduff for twenty-five years there were still some people living locally that I didn't get to know. These are brief sketches of those I did. And they are all mostly dead now.

Hawkins

Our closest neighbours were the Hawkins'. They lived at the crossroads at Clondaw in a tiny thatched cottage attached to their yard. In this basic house Samuel and Evelyn (Evie) raised their family of three sons named Thomas, Victor and Mervyn. Many years later they built a modern bungalow next door. The thatch on the old house was removed and replaced with corrugated iron sheets and it was then used for storage.

Samuel or Sam was a small, likable pipe-smoking man. He walked with a pronounced limp the result of a motorcycle accident sustained as a young man. The broken femur had apparently never been reset properly. He also had an untreated bunion which meant all his shoes and boots couldn't be worn without first cutting a hole into the upper. Sam had evidently been a bit of a tearaway in his youth. Dan often talked about their exploits and would frequently refer to him a 'Iron Sam' which I assumed was because of his toughness. It was only much later that I realized that what Dan was actually saying was 'I and Sam'.

After a short illness Sam passed away in the bed, he'd slept in all his life. When the undertaker, one Dan Laffan finally arrived late in the evening he was very much the worse for drink having spent the day in Harney's Pub in Ballyedmond. Because the house was so small it was discovered after much pushing and shoving that it was not possible to get the coffin into the room where Sam reposed. After a long and noisy debate between the mortician, his assistant and the family it was decided that the only solution was to pass the body out through the window. And so it was that poor Sam made his final, undignified exit from the family home accompanied by a lot of grunting, swearing and laughter.

Evie – short for Evelyn was a kindly woman who worked incredibly hard. She did most of the yard work like milking the cows and goats, and feeding and bedding the animals, as well as the cooking and cleaning and raising three boys. Because of Sam's disability he wasn't able to do a lot to help. Throughout her life she always maintained a cheerful demeanour despite tragically losing a husband, two sons, and a daughter-in-law.

Thomas was the eldest of the three sons and never married. He was not exactly lazy but he never over exerted himself either. He spent a lot of time in the pub in Monogear drinking with Father Jim Grennan. He owned and operated a JCB tractor digger which he used for hire work whenever he was contacted by a client; he never went out looking for work. He also had a hedge trimmer attachment which he hired out as well whenever he had no work for the digger; but again, he never killed himself seeking work. He was very casual about getting paid for the work he did do. It could be weeks before he'd present an invoice for payment, usually written on a scrap of paper. He was content to work for his meals provided by whomever he happened to be working for. He was a lifelong smoker (his cigarette of choice being Majors) and eventually he succumbed to an early death due to heart problems.

Victor was married with two daughters; Sandra and Pauline. His first wife Fiona died relatively young and he remarried. He was just the opposite of Thomas. He owned a garage at the end of the land at Garryduff where he repaired farm machinery and cars. He also held a franchise for chainsaws and lawnmowers. He could be incredibly grumpy and rude, and if it hadn't been so convenient to use his services, I don't think I would have gone to him. (But as Cass used to say whenever something broke "Zickter will six it.") Unlike Thomas, Victor presented his bill at the same time as you collected whatever he'd repaired and he charged for every last nut and bolt, plus his time, which I often suspected he inflated. He suffered from asthma and eczema (which he pronounced 'egzeemah'). If you happened to be at his garage when he was suffering the most recent onslaught of the disease, he'd unashamedly lift his shirt to reveal the latest outbreak of spots and blisters – gross. Victor died at a relatively young age too.

Mervyn – 'Merv the Serve' (so called because of his practice of driving everywhere flat out) was still at school when we first became acquainted with the Hawkins'. He left as soon as he was able and worked on their small farm. He was very hard working and as soon as he had saved enough money, he bought himself a Massey-Ferguson 390 tractor and did hire work to supplement the farm income. (Sam's little grey Ferguson tractor wasn't big enough). He could be extremely precocious and a bit of a know-it-all. Dan would often be exasperated with his attitude and be delighted when he did something wrong or he broke something. Mervyn married a local girl and when we left, he had two small children.

Kelly

Living on the opposite side of Cross at Clondaw to the Hawkins' were the Kelly's. Mr Kelly (whom I never really got to know), Mrs Kelly, a nice sociable, rotund woman and their son Dick. Dick was a young man (in his early thirties) who suffered with an excruciating stutter. When his father died, he inherited the farm, along with the all the livestock and machinery. At that time the farm was a viable concern providing a living for the family. But Dick had a problem; as well as being a lazy good-for-nothing he was a compulsive gambler. In the space of about five years, he sold off the cattle, and then the tractors and machinery. After his mother died, he sold the land too. Finally, when there was nothing else left, he sold the slates off the roof of the dwelling house leaving it to fall into dereliction, all to feed his addiction. He disappeared from the area soon after this and rumours later surfaced that he had moved to London and been hospitalized with broken legs.

Guest

Eddie (Edward) and Jessie (Jessica) Guest and their son Henry farmed land that adjoined Garryduff. It had in fact been part off Garryduff many years ago when Lady Geary owned the land. Their house was named Garryduff Villa. Henry had been born with Down's syndrome and sadly died when he was only 18. Eddie's brother Willie (William) also lived with them. He was a cadaverous looking man who had something wrong with his back which caused him to walk with a curious listing gait and necessitated him having to wear a leather corset for support. Unfortunately, whenever he moved the thing creaked like a galleon under sail.

Webster

The Websters were once a large and important family who owned Garrybrit, an adjoining townland to Garryduff. When we arrived, they were all elderly and only a few of the family remained. The survivors all lived together in the big house. There was Henry, Ned (Edward), Annie and Sissy. (I never discovered her true name; she was always known as Sissy because she was the youngest sister). They all died whilst we were there and Garrybrit was sold to Padder (Patrick) Lacey. There was also a younger Webster brother, Jim, who was married to Dolly (Dorothy) Webster nee Black. They lived in a bungalow built on their land. Jim was the only Webster to marry and when he died childless the family died out.

Mulrennen

Patrick and Mary Mulrennen and their two daughters, Sandra and Diane at one time lived in the old Glebe House at Kilcormick. (Dan always pronounced it as the Glebby). The house had originally been the rectory for the parish but like so many others the upkeep had become too expensive and Church had sold it off. It had had several occupants before the Mulrennen's took up residence. The family moved house fairly often and they only lived in the Glebe for a few years before they moved on. Diane and Cass were in school together and remain great friends who still stay in touch. Diane married and moved to Dublin then to Dubai where her husband Paul worked for Microsoft before returning to live in Naas. Pat was an enthusiastic race-goer and would drive all over the country in his Volvo 145 Estate car to attend meetings. Mary was an extremely thin woman about whom it was said that all she ever ate were Twix bars, but I don't believe this. Sandra qualified as a nurse and moved to England to work. After Pat died and the daughters moved way Mary built herself a small bungalow where she lives still, so far as I know.

Furlong

Living in one of the ubiquitous Council two-up-two-down cottages in Ballincash were Nick (Nicolas) and Nancy (Ann) Furlong with their two daughters Mary and Eileen. I employed the girls during the raspberry picking season. Both girls were assiduous and tireless workers unlike

Diane Mulrennen who ate most of what she picked. They also occasionally baby-sat for us. Nick was a younger brother of Dan.

Redmond

Further along the same road in Ballincash was the Redmond's farm. I only knew Pierce or Pierrie as he was known but he had a large family as well as two brother who also lived in the house. The brothers were Mikey, who was somewhat mentally deficient (or one should say had learning difficulties) and Phillip. Pierrie was an unlucky man. First his hayshed caught fire completely incinerating his stock of winter fodder and also destroying his adjoining milking parlour. A few years later the dwelling house also caught fire and burned to the ground leaving the family homeless. All the local neighbours rallied round and arranged accommodation for the family members until the house could be re-built.

Pierre's brother Phillip ran the general store at Raheenduff and not being a man who trusted banks he kept all the cash from the business, about £14,000 at the time in a tin box which was lost in the fire.

Phillip's shop at Reheenduff was a general store, a grocery and a pub, and it was not uncommon to see people standing at the counter drinking pints of Guinness. Phil sold pretty much anything, from hardware, dried goods, feedstuffs, meat and vegetables, milk and dairy products as well as beer and spirits. If one wanted some bacon, Phil would carve a joint from the side of a pig which would be hanging in the corner of the shop. He would butcher it on the top of an old battered ice-cream freezer. In the summer time the meat would frequently be crawling with maggots which Phil would wipe off with a piece of hessian sacking before cutting it up. (The Department for Health and Safety were not as zealous then as they are today). And people were less squeamish in those days too. The meat would be cooked anyway, usually boiled and any bacterium or salmonella would be killed making it safe to eat.

Grady

Further along the same road on which the Redmond's lived was Willy Grady in another of the little council cottages. He was an elderly, single man who barely survived on what he could grow on the half acre of land that came with the cottage. He owned an elderly cow which he grazed on the grass verges at the road side – what was colloquially known as the 'Long Acre'. He often bought hay from me. I was reluctant to charge him but he always insisted on paying the going rate.

Fortune

Jim and Pat Fortune were two brothers who lived in neighbouring houses that were equally run down and in a state of disrepair. Pat was universally known as Bun; I know not why. Each of the brothers had large families; Jim had 10 and Bun had 12 kids. Bun fell afoul of the Board of Education as his house was just outside the boundary line that would qualify his children for free school transport, so he built a tin shed that was inside the limit and claimed this to be his domicile and therefore he now qualified. The Department for Education did not agree.

Jim was a quiet, likeable man but a bit of a rogue. He would haggle for ages over the price of a bale of hay or straw and I usually gave in to him. He still owes me for 80 bales of hay he never paid for.

Rath

Willie was the oldest Rath and lived with his identical twin brothers Leonard and Francie (I could never tell them apart). They lived and farmed together at Ballincash Upper. They were all extremely talented mechanics. Except for the tractors they made all their agricultural machinery themselves. They'd surreptitiously make drawings or photograph the piece of equipment they needed then go to their workshop and build it from any scrap iron or steel they happened to have. They attended St Cormac's church and were all bachelors. Another family destined for extinction.

Dowd

Patrick Dowd was another man I frequently did business with. He was very tall and erect; he always wore a necktie whatever the weather despite his shirt and jacket being threadbare. He was inevitably unshaven with unkempt hair. Pat's dwelling house also burned down at some time in the past and the family moved into a barn where they lived for several years till a new house could be built. He too had a large family and was relatively poor but he never haggled over prices and paid whatever was asked. Like a lot of country folk of his generation he was semi-illiterate and when it came time to pay for items, they would simply hand over their cheque book for the seller or shopkeeper to write out the amount, they would then sign it with a carefully practiced signature.

Nolan

Garryduff was sold in 1995 and in the summer of that year we moved to a house at Ballynastraw in Glenbrien. Eamon Nolan our new neighbour was an extremely hard-working young man who milked a herd of 120 dairy cows. His family had lived and farmed here from long before any of the surrounding houses were built and the area had become settled. Never-the-less, Eamon continued to farm as he'd always done, making no concessions for the people who now lived near him. Twice a day during the spring, summer and autumn he would drive his herd of cows along the communal lane where they deposited large quantities of slurry onto the road, much to the considerable annoyance of all the residents who used the lane. He obstinately refused to change his methods despite the many and repeated appeals that he move his cows by a different route. The battle was still ongoing when we left the area 10 years later.

We named the house at Ballynastraw – 'Tristenagh'. It was a huge barracks of a place with about 20 acres of land which we needed for Miss Mitchell (our remaining horse) and her companion pony Melody to graze on. Our predecessor had bult the house himself. He didn't appear to have followed any plans or blue-prints but had simply made it up as he went along. From the original starting point he had added extensions to each end of the building, one of which was still incomplete when we moved in. Soon after our arrival I discovered that the seals on the double glazing had failed in a lot of the windows allowing them to fog up with condensation between the panes of glass, so I decided to get them replaced. When I measured the windows, I found to my astonishment that everyone was a different size. It seems that the original owner had built the house around the windows rather than fitting the window into the house. I guess he must have bought them as a job lot from somewhere.

When James and Cass had left home to start their own lives, we found that Tristenegh was too big for just the two of us. Melody had died and Miss Mitchell was boarded with Paddy Bolger so the need for grazing was no longer necessary without any livestock. During this period the Department of Agriculture had introduced a scheme of encouraging farmers to establish forestry plantations and for doing this a grant was paid to compensate for the loss of income from the land for the following 20 years. To take advantage of this I planted a mixture of Sitka Spruce, Lodgepole Pine and Ash trees on ten acres of the land to which I retained ownership, the remainder was sold with the house.

When we left, the property was sold to John Vance and his wife.

Doran

We moved again in 2005 to a small bungalow named 'Derravaragh' in Barntown, just outside

Wexford town and our new neighbours were Brendan and Carmel Doran. They were a nice couple who had lived there since Brendan built the house back in the 70's. Over the years he'd built all sorts of other ramshackle sheds and shacks to house his horses, pigs, calves and chickens, and now the place looked like a shanty town. It was also an attractive breeding ground for rats which occasionally found their way onto our property, but only ever made it into the house once.

Brendan never seemed to hold a 'proper' job with paid employment but survived doing odd jobs whenever and wherever he could find them. On several occasions I paid him to do work for me and although he was a bit slap-dash his work was reasonably good. He was a jovial sort of man and was most obliging; he'd do anything for you; nothing was too much trouble.

One of the many feral cats that lived around the area and that Carmel had adopted bit Brendan on the index finger of his right hand when he tried to pick it up. The finger became infected and eventually turned gangrenous and had unfortunately to be amputated from the second knuckle. Moral – leave stray cats alone.

We moved to Barntown because we wanted somewhere smaller to live; to down-size in the jargon. Although Derravaragh was perfectly adequate for our needs, we decided that we needed a bigger kitchen and Anna wanted an en-suite bathroom in the master bedroom, so we built on extensions. This didn't turn out to be as simple, or as cheap as we'd anticipated. The planning authorities in Wexford insisted that before permission to build was granted we would have to install a new bio sustainable septic tank (we were not connected to the mains sewer) and because this was sited too close to the existing well, (we were not connected to mains water either) we were required to bore a new one which all added considerably to the cost. But when the work was completed, we had a very comfortable house which we both loved. It was the house in which Anna died and which I reluctantly sold a year later.

Builders – Paddy and Michael

Patrick (Paddy) Jennings and Michael Heffernan were a two-man building operation who over the years did a lot of work at Garryduff and who consequently we became great friends with. Paddy assumed the role of boss and chief negotiator whilst Michael was the craftsman doing all the skilled work. Paddy did the labouring work like mixing the cement and carrying bricks etc.

Paddy was a small wiry man whilst Michael was the opposite, standing over six feet tall and solidly built. Paddy was a forty a day smoker, his brand of choice being Embassy Blue cigarettes. He also had the rottenest teeth I've ever seen in a human mouth; his entire upper and lower front teeth were black with decay. I suspect his other teeth were the same. I'd wince as I watched him sucking on his fags; the thought of the cold air being dragged into his mouth over his rotten teeth made me shudder.

He was an amusing man who had a great love of horses. Being small of stature he was the idea size and weight to be a jockey, and he regularly rode his horses at point-to-point meetings. He owed several race horses and hunters over the years I knew him. He rarely won a race, but that didn't matter to Paddy, it was the excitement that he loved. He drove an old beat-up Datsun Cherry car with which he towed his horsebox; a car that was woefully underpowered for the job. The risk of it breaking down never seemed to worry Paddy though.

He lived with his wife Marion in a little two-up-two-down council cottage at Kilpierce onto which he had built a toilet and a bathroom. They raised six children in it. (Not particularly unusual for the time; Dan Furlong had been one of nine reared in a similar house but without indoor plumbing). They had three boys and three girls namely - P.J. (Patrick Joseph), Carmel, Kaye, Tracy and Sean. The last child Roy was either an afterthought or a mistake as he was born 10 years after Sean. Later Michael Heffernan would marry the oldest girl, Carmel; the fate of the remainder is not known, but I'm sure they're all married with families by now.

There are records of Garryduff being extant in 1840 and it's safe to assume that the original structure was built many years before then. Old buildings such as Garryduff House require constant maintenance and could very easily become a money-pit. So, it was also inevitable that Paddy and Michael would be frequent visitors to carry out work not only on the house but also on the old stone out-buildings.

Paddy and Michael had the annoying practice (as did many small builders in Ireland) of starting a job and then disappearing for days or even weeks while they worked on other jobs. There seemed to be an unwritten code among the building fraternity that no one would take on work that had been started by someone else, so we'd just have to wait until they returned. They did many jobs at Garryduff over the years and on every occasion, they did the same thing – much to my annoyance and frustration. But by employing them to do the work one just had to accept that this was going to happen.

Another habit they had, and it took me a while to cop on to it, was that whenever I went to speak to them, they would both immediately stop whatever they were doing and would happily talk, not resuming the work until I left. After all they reasoned, I was paying for their time so, if I wanted to spend it talking then that was okay with them. So, I had to desist and restrict conversations to lunch breaks, which was a pity as I enjoyed the banter and they were a great source of gossip.

Unsurprisingly though, during the course of whatever work they were doing they would discover further 'vital' work that needed to be done as well. Like the time they were to remove a redundant slate water tank from outside the kitchen window. This led to the discovery that the wall behind the tank would have to be stripped and re-plastered, the gable wall would also require repairing and a window would have to be replaced etcetera etcetera. A halt had to be called before the list of work got too long.

At some time during the Binnions' era, Henry had decided to replace the original kitchen window with a much larger one. From evidence gleaned from previous work he'd undertaken it was clear that he was no craftsman, rather an enthusiastic do-it-yourself bodger. (The central heating system he'd installed for example was a complete disaster and never worked properly). Rather than support the weight of the wall above the new window with an RSJ spanning the opening as should have been done, he'd instead used a length of steel pipe to prop up the entire gable end of the house. When it was removed it turned out to be an old propeller shaft from a car. It was a mystery as to how the wall had stayed up for so many years, but when cracks started to appear, it was decided that a proper repair would have to be done. So, summon Paddy and Michael.

A few weeks later they arrived in their old car towing a trailer with their cement mixer and shovels etc ready to start the job. I went out to meet them and was greeted by a grinning Paddy flashing an array of sparkling white teeth. He'd finally had the rotten ones extracted and been fitted with a set of shiny new gnashers. He confessed that he'd dreaded going to a dentist but the pain and finally become so unbearable that he'd been forced to bite the bullet.

To complete this job entailed the removal of the old window and a lot of the gable end wall leaving the kitchen exposed to the elements. Thankfully this was during the summer and was the one occasion that they stayed till the work was completed. They did concede that they couldn't very well leave us with the kitchen in bits as we spent most of our time in it. The house felt a lot safer after the job was finished.

At some time in the distant past a previous owner had built an ugly square section onto the front of the house. This had enlarged the entrance hall on the ground floor and provided a bathroom above. On the roof of the bathroom was a large concrete tank which supplied water to the toilet (running water was a new innovation for the time) but it had cracked and begun to leak into the rooms below. After a visit by Sammy Deane, a friend of Leslie's who was an architect, they concluded that the house would look much better if the square front was demolished and replaced with a Georgian façade featuring a semi-circular fanlight above a widened front door. It would mean that the hall would be smaller and the bathroom above would need re-designing to allow for the smaller area. Here was another job for Paddy and Michael.

A week or so into the job the lads turned up for work as usual with Paddy looking like he'd done ten rounds in the ring with Mike Tyson. (World heavyweight boxing champion at the time). He sported two black eyes and a swollen nose with a cut across the bridge of it. I asked him what the hell had happened and he explained that he had gone to J. Donohue's Railway Stores in

Enniscorthy to collect fifteen feet of 4-inch plastic sewer pipe that they needed for the new bathroom. He didn't have his trailer with him and the only way he could get the pipe into the car was diagonally across the inside with about five feet sticking out of the passenger side window. This was fine until he was forced to steer into the side of the road to avoid an oncoming tractor loaded with hay. Unfortunately, the protruding end of the pipe caught in the hedge and was forced backwards. Obeying Newton's third law of motion, the other end of the pipe was propelled forwards at 40 miles and hour cracking Paddy on the back of his head opening a gash that required 4 stitches, at the same time smashing his face onto the steering wheel causing his facial injuries. (No seat belt of course). Luckily, he didn't pass out and had the presence of mind to apply the brakes and so didn't crash the car. The pipe however, was rendered useless being spilt and bent at the pivot point. He returned the next day with two shorter lengths and a joiner which he could safely get inside the car.

They did a very good job though, and the house looked far more attractive for it. It subsequently became my annual chore to paint the front of the house with a yellow ochre wash.

The first time we met the pair of them was when we arrived from England to take up residence. They were laying concrete floors and dry-lining the drawing and dining rooms. (Which was the reason we were confined to the kitchen as the remainder of the house was uninhabitable). To facilitate this work required the removal of the two large black-marble fireplaces that were installed in the rooms. It was a simple enough job to dismantle them but over the several weeks that the work took to do, the 50 or 60 separate pieces got mixed up and were moved about several times. Some of larger parts got broken during the time they were in pieces and a couple of smaller bits got lost. When it came time to put them back together, neither Paddy nor Michael could remember exactly how the jig-saw puzzle should be assembled. Consequently, the fireplaces always looked a bit cock-eyed and slightly out of true; and certain pieces didn't fit together properly. One part had even been reinstalled back-to-front. Forever afterward it irritated me whenever I contemplated them. They were a constant reminder of Paddy and Michael.

We lost touch with them after we moved from Garryduff to Glenbrien. I suppose Paddy must have died after all this time and Michael must be retired. He was much younger than Paddy; I think he was about the same age as me.

Dogs Cats and other Animals

Over the years we owned many dogs and cats. Garryduff was an ideal place to keep pets as there were acres of land for them to run on, and plenty of vermin for the cats. The dogs detailed here stretched over a period of 40 years and three homes. Most of them died of old age. The last one, Molly dying in 2012.

Baker

Baker was the first dog we owned. We purchased him after we'd been in Garryduff for about six months. He was a big handsome Black Labrador. Anna located him somewhere in Dublin and he came to us as a 12-week-old puppy. Unfortunately, as Baker grew, he revealed a darker side to his character: he chased sheep. This is of course an absolute no-no for dogs in a farming community (or anywhere else for that matter). We were unaware that he did this until a neighbour; John Donohue came to the house and complained. He has seen the dog several times running after his flock and now felt constrained to say something as two of his ewes (always pronounced as Yows in Ireland) had aborted their lambs. He knew that the dog belonged to us as he had followed it back to the house. Mr Donohue regretted to insist that we must get rid of the dog or, he implied, a prosecution would be forthcoming.

There was really only one option for us; Baker would have to be put down. We couldn't give him away because once a sheep chaser always a sheep chaser, and we could find no-one who'd take him in town. At the time there was a lot of reports – and photographs in 'The Echo' newspaper of the damage packs of roaming dogs had done to flocks of sheep, so there was quite a lot of ill feeling towards dog owners.

On the fateful day I shut Baker into one of the stables and waited for Martin Kent to come and administer the euthanasia jab. It broke my heart when I returned to the stable, opened the door and found the dog lying with his nose pressed to the gap at the bottom of the door waiting faithfully for me to come back. I buried him in the orchard and was in floods tears as I did so. To this day I choke up whenever I think of it.

Florence

Florrie was a Golden Cocker Spaniel bitch who we acquired to replace Baker. She was a sweet, loveable, good-natured dog who unlike Baker never strayed from the land. Rather than chase sheep she was afraid of them and would run away as soon as one looked at her. But she was totally disobedient and would not do what she was told. If called, she would stop, turn and look at you, consider the order and then continue on with her original purpose. She lived for many years but eventually she developed a cancerous growth between the toes of her front foot which required an amputation and which precipitated her final demise.

Jess

Jess was another Golden Cocker. We got her as a Christmas present for Cass who for some time had expressed a desire for a dog of her own. Whilst James and Cass were opening their stockings sitting on our bed on Christmas morning (as was our tradition) I nipped down stairs and collected the pup from where she was hidden. I put her in a cardboard box and wrapped it in Christmas paper then presented it to Cass. The child was flabbergasted and delighted when a little pup jumped out of the box into her arms. Jess was a crafty (or should I say clever) dog who discovered it was possible to open the fridge door and steal the contents, she also learned to close the door. I caught her red-handed during one such raid and put a stop to the practice by fixing child safety locks to the door to stop her.

Sadie

A Dalmatian. I can't remember where Sadie came from but she was the runt of the litter and was poorly marked for a Dalmatian. She was therefore not good enough to show or breed from, so we got her for nothing. She was a nervous sort of animal and not very brave. She died aged 11.

Timmy

Timmy as the sole survivor from Sadie's only litter. I have no knowledge of when or by whom she became pregnant. It was a difficult labour for the dog that the Vet had to eventually induce. After the birth we were advised to have her spayed as any further pregnancies could prove fatal for the dog. She gave birth to four pups, two were still-born and one died soon after the birth. Timmy grew into a fine big dog with Dalmatian spots, a Sheep dogs ruff and a course coat. At some time as a pup, he acquired a distinctive notch in one ear.

One morning I let Timmy out as usual for a run and do his business but he never returned. We searched high and low, asked all the neighbours if they had seen him. I placed a notice in 'The Echo' newspaper and posted flyers everywhere but no sign was ever seen of the dog again. He had simply disappeared. I worried that he might have been caught in a snare and died horribly. Setting snares was a common practice at the time for catching foxes for which the Department of Agriculture paid a bounty.

In the end after extensive searching over many days we concluded that he had been taken (dog napped?) by Travellers. They were known to do this if they came across an unaccompanied dog and to sell the them later in some other part of the country. I hope that this was his fate and he hadn't been killed on the road and his body dumped.

Moppie

Moppie was an elderly Cocker Spaniel that Anna rescued after she had been abandoned out in the country. This was a fairly common occurrence when a dog had gotten too old and the owners no longer wanted it. Driving back from Enniscorthy one day she came across the dog pathetically running after cars desperately trying to find her owner. Anna enquired at all the nearby houses but no one could identify the dog or claim ownership so Anna had no alternative but bring the dog home. Moppie (a name we dubbed her because of her heavy shaggy coat; she looked like a floor mop) happily settled in with the other dogs. The poor thing had been horribly neglected, she was filthy dirty and alive with fleas. He coat was extremely matted and I spent many hours with the dog on my lap clipping the knots out of her fur. She was delighted to receive the attention.

She lived with us for over a year before ill health overcame her. Her back legs became paralysed forcing her to drag herself around the kitchen on her bottom but when she became incontinent, we were forced to bring her into the Vets to be put down. Always a sad thing to do but at least her last few months were happy.

Nellie

Nellie was another stray we took in. She was a Jack Russell that James found one day cowering and shivering under a hedge. She had clearly been thrown out and dumped in the country. Another case of someone no longer wanting her. The poor thing was starving and crawling with fleas. Her right fore-leg had been broken at some time in the past and had not been reset properly so that it stuck out at an odd angle. She recovered quickly from the trauma of abandonment and was soon ruling the house. Regrettably, she developed diabetes that was untreatable and terminal so we decided to have her put down before she became too ill and in too much pain. Like Moppie her last few years were happy. She was a devoted and faithful dog; who turned out to be an excellent ratter and the source of endless entertainment to all of us.

Sally

Sally was another Dalmatian. I cannot remember from where she came only that we got her as a pup. She lived for 11 or 12 years finally dying of old age.

Lilly

Lilly came to us after a photograph appeared on the front page of the 'Irish Times' of a young girl holding six pups in her arms. The ISPCA was appealing for homes for the pups after they had been found abandoned. Anna immediately phoned and volunteered to take one. Lilly turned out to one of those universal mongrels that can be seen all over the world scavenging in bins and roaming in packs. She was still a little bit untamed and she never really became as friendly and loving as the other dogs we'd owned – she didn't like to be fondled or fussed over and I never fully trusted her.

Molly

Molly was our last dog. She was mostly Jack Russell but black and her mother was a Dachshund. A friend of Anna's owned the mother so there was no doubting her maternal side. Whoever the father was remained a mystery. Anna gave her to me as a birthday present and as a replacement for Nellie who'd recently died and whom I missed. She was a sweet little dog, not as characterful as Nellie but never-the-less loveable. She died naturally of old age being 14 at the time.

Cats

During our time at Garryduff there were only ever three cats, who were all males. We only knew where one came from, the others came with the farm and always seemed to have been around. Being males, we avoided Mrs Dan's problem of them inter-breeding and the numbers becoming a problem. No doubt our cats also visited Mrs Dan's as I often recognized a similar looking animal.

George was a black and white cat who lived mostly in the yard only coming to the house for food. His origins were known as he was found as a kitten hiding in the engine of our car. How he came to be there is a mystery. Anna had brought the children to Kilnamanagh School and when she returned home, she heard a weak mewing coming from under the bonnet. On investigation the little thing was discovered huddled against the engine hanging on for dear life. This was much like the human equivalent of a stowaway hiding in the landing gear of a jet aircraft. For some reason *George* was frequently afflicted with ear mites and the only way to treat them was to bathe the cat in a solution of insecticide – not an easy operation considering a cat's aversion to water.

The other two were *Henry*, a grey tabby and *Oscar* a marmalade cat. *Oscar* also discovered that if a carton of milk had been left out it was a simple matter to knock it over and get a drink - and make a frightful mess as well. None of these cats were in anyway loveable and as they died or disappeared, we didn't replace them as neither Anna nor I were particularly fond of cats. They were tolerated as vermin control operatives.

Horses

Over the years many horses lived at Garryduff, and I'm afraid I can't remember them all. The ones that I can remember were:

Jolane, Bay mare
Avril Blake, Bay mare
Salt, Chestnut mare
Karayasha, Chestnut mare
Symingia, Bay mare
Godskiss, Grey mare (we called her *Mary*)
Miss Mitchel Grey filly
Melody Bay pony
Joxer Bay pony
Scott Connemara Cob

Karayasha belonged to Anna and was bought from the Aga Khan's Stud in Co. Kildare.

They were all thoroughbred broodmares (except Miss Mitchel and the ponies) whose sole purpose was the breeding of foals. The gestation period for a horse is about 11 months, so just before a mare was due to foal, she would be sent off to the stud farm where she'd give birth and then immediately be covered by the stallion selected for her next offspring. (Hopefully a colt).

When the foaling was imminent the mare would be loaded into the horse-box and Anna and I or occasionally Dan, would set off towing it with our old Land Rover that had seen better days. The vehicle was extremely underpowered, (it didn't have the grunt to pull the skin off a rice pudding) and make our slow way to County Tipperary or County Meath or wherever the stud farm happened to be. We later exchanged the Landy for a Volkswagen Passat which wasn't a great improvement. A couple of months later we would return to the stud farm and collect the horse and her baby. Hopefully the mare would be in foal again.

Their offspring were offered for sale at Goff's or Tattersalls Bloodstock sales where they were sold as either foals or yearlings. They aren't officially named till later in life when they began their racing careers and their names are registered with Wetherbys.

We raced several horses at various racetracks in Ireland with varying degrees of success. A horse named *Twentynineagain* won a race at Roscommon, but by far the most successful was undoubtedly *Miss Mitchell.* She won a number of races including the Leopardstown November Handicap. She was trained by Richard Lister at his stables at Coolgreany in north county Wexford. She was a grey filly who came to stay with us when she retired from racing.

Melody and *Joxer* were two ponies which were used mainly as companion horses. Originally Anna used to ride *Joxer* for hunting until she gave it up. *Melody* was purchased for Cass when she was going through her pony stage and who had expressed an interest in riding. There were also a couple of donkeys named *Clem* and *Winston* who had no purpose but to be seen and occasionally keep a foal company after it had been weened.

Scott was a Connemara Cob gelding that Leslie rode when he hunted with the Bray Harriers and sometime with the Island Hunt. The horse came to Garryduff from Fey Yerra when Leslie gave up hunting and it lived out its days with us.

Karayasha's end sadly came when she developed a severe case of laminitis in both of her front hooves. It got so bad that the poor horse was eventually unable to walk. Three or four times a day I would bathe her feet in cold water hoping to relieve some of the pain. Finally, it was decided that the humane thing to do was to put her down. Michael O'Shea came out and shot her. Unfortunately, the insurance company insisted on retaining evidence of the malaise, so Michael was obliged to amputate her legs from the knee. To keep them safe, I wrapped them in plastic bags and stored them in the freezer. (Much to Anna and Cass's abhorrence).

As the horses became too old to breed or got ill it was often necessary to have then put down. I hated to have to do this. I would always corral them in a paddock or a loose box which was familiar to them, and this way they'd be relaxed and not unduly stressed. I couldn't bear the thought of sending them to the factory as so many other owners did. Martin Kent would place the .45 Webley revolver between their eyes and fire a shot into their brain. Death was instantaneous. The spark of life simply vanished from their eyes and they were dead before they hit the ground. I usually donated the carcass to the Island hunt who butchered, rendered and fed the meat to their foxhounds.

There is something very poignant and upsetting in the faith and trust a horse has for you. They will stand quietly beside you completely unaware of what is about to befall them. You can see the recognition and trust in their eyes as you hold the head-collars and stoke their muzzles for the last time. It can be very distressing. I once asked Martin if it ever got any easier when he had to shoot them – his one-word answer - No.

Miscellaneous Others

As James grew up, he developed an interest in birds. His interest started with the ducks that lived on the pond in the yard. There were a mix of breeds, - Aylesbury's, Rouen's, Mallards, Muscovy's and Bombay Runner's. (The numbers had built up again after Nubbins disastrous massacre.) One duck of note was a large male Muscovy drake named *Freddie*. (We named it after the character Freddie Kruger in a film 'Nightmare on Elm Street'). The bird was very aggressive and would attack and hiss at anyone who got too close to it. The thing came to Garryduff after a report on the radio said that there was a wild duck loose on the road in

Greystones (a town near Dublin) that no one could catch and no one seemed to own. The bird was penned in someone's garden and if anyone was willing to collect it, they could have it. Anna immediately drove to Greystones with James and they brought it back. He lived with us for quite a while before unfortunately coming to a sad end. He attacked a vehicle that had driven into the yard, but the driver didn't see him and poor *Freddie* perished under the wheels of the car.

From ducks his interest expanded into chickens. He kept a lot of bantams of many different breeds including Silkies, Leghorns and Old English Game. One of them was a Nanking Bantam Cockerel who he named *Rufus*. The bird had a habit of flying up onto the kitchen window-sill and pecking on the glass to get attention. When the window was opened, he'd march in and strut up and down the worktops thrusting his chest out like an army sergeant major and crowing. Everyone loved *Rufus*. James' interest then turned to ornamental pheasants. I don't recall all the different species he kept but among them were Golden, Silver, Lady Amherst, and Reeves pheasants and many others. To house all these birds required the building of pens in the orchard; a substantial undertaking I may say. His hobby also involved me driving James all over the country to visit other enthusiasts and to buy and sell birds.

At one time we reared an orphan lamb named *Biddy*. It was bottle fed it in the kitchen which was not a problem until it grew too big and then had a habit of bunting the children knocking them over when it was looking for food. It also made a mess on the floor not being house trained. It finally went to the abattoir.

Cass had a passion for gerbils at one time. She liked having them in her bedroom because they masked the noise of the mice running about under the floor boards and in the ceiling. When these died her interest turned to Hamsters. Never being sure what sex they were, Cass housed males and females together and woke up one morning to discover a nest of babies. They proliferated at an alarming rate and I was pushed to construct new boxes in which to house them all. The mother of the third generation turned out to be a cannibal who ate her babies. One of the second-generation litter had a habit of placing its rear end against the bars of its cage and squirting its pee out into the room. In the end there were so many that Cass went into business selling them to pet shops.

I recall one occasion when Cass was playing with her favourite hamster in the kitchen and it escaped. Appropriately she had named it Houdini. It was last seen disappearing down the gap between the wall and the worktop. I had to dismantling one of the kitchen units in an attempt to recapture but it couldn't be found. Several weeks later it suddenly reappeared in the kitchen. It was caught and returned to its cage. It must have lived with the mice because it was in good health and well fed.

Cass also kept a Guinea Pig at one time. If it had a name, I've forgotten it. It too escaped but before it could be caught *Oscar* found it and killed it.

Foreign Holidays

Although foreign holidays are not strictly memories of living in Ireland they are never-the-less an integral part of our family life, and as such I've included some of them here.

Anna got the travel bug once we moved from Garryduff to Glenbrien. As we no longer had the responsibility for looking after animals, (the dogs could be put in kennels) we were now free to holiday abroad. Having travelled extensively during my days in the Royal Navy I wasn't as mad to go exploring the world as Anna. She had only ever been to Oslo in Norway as a teenager and she wanted to broaden her horizons.

Mediterranean

Our first trip abroad was to Cyprus. We stayed in the Hotel Capitano near Larnaca and on a second holiday to Cyprus a year or so later we stayed at a place near Paphos. We holidayed in Spain staying in a rental apartment at Nerja near Malaga. We spent a week in Fuerteventura and Lanzarote in the Canary Islands and on another occasion, we took a Mediterranean Cruise starting and finishing in Majorca. Among other places the cruise called at were Naples, Sicily and Barcelona. One of my bucket-list places to see was Pompei which is only a short distance from Naples. I was terribly disappointed when we finally got there as the place was so crowded that it was difficult to see anything. Docked in Naples at the same time as us were several other cruise ships (including the QEII) and all of their passengers seemed to be in Pompei at the same time as we were. I don't remember in which order we did these trips nor can I remember the dates but it seemed as if we were no sooner back from one trip than Anna was planning the next. It sometimes felt as if we didn't have time to unpack our suitcases.

Peru

In 2003/04 we did our first long trip which was to Peru. Cass was living and working in Santiago, Chile at the time as a language teacher and she flew to Lima to meet us. She was invaluable as our travel guide and interpreter. After a few days in Miraflores to acclimatize we flew to Cuzco, altitude 11000 feet, where we stayed in a lovely hacienda type hotel. I got to drink a lot of matte, a concoction made from stewed cocoa leaves that is said to be good for altitude sickness.

From Cuzco Cass booked us onto a local bus that took us to Pisac, a small town at the head of the Sacred Valley. To get there was one of the scariest bus rides I ever took. The old banger of a bus rattled and belched out clouds of acrid smoke as it rolled along. At every stop more and more people crammed on, until I didn't believe it was possible to get any more passengers onto a bus. I found myself crushed between ethnic travellers who would definitely have benefitted from a shower. Anna and the kids somehow managed to secure seats. The road zigzagged down the mountain to the valley floor with precipitous drops on each side of the road. There were many wrecks visible at the bottom of the cliffs. It was made scarier because of the doubtful roadworthiness of the vehicle and the overcrowding.

We stayed in a terrible hotel overlooking the Plaza de Mayor in Pisac. The building was in desperate need of repair and during the night a heavy rain storm flooded our rooms putting us all in danger due to the dodgy state of the exposed electrical wiring. We ate at a restaurant that served some of the worse food I ever ate. I wrapped the piece of meat that purported to be a steak (it was probably Llama or some other unidentified mammal.) in a tissue and threw it to the mangy town dogs and even they were reluctant to eat it!

The next day we took a taxi to Ollantaytambo. The taxi was a beat-up old wreck of a car, which seem to be the standard norm for taxis in Pisac. The driver was obliged to make frequent stops to check on the back wheel nuts which were in danger of coming undone and falling off; a bit disconcerting. That night we hostelled in Ollantaytambo then got a train the next morning to Aquas-Calientes, which is the jumping off place for Machu Picchu. We vacated our lodgings early the next morning so as to get to Machu Picchu before the crowds built up. We travelled in a minibus (you could hike if you were feeling fit and strong) and drove up a winding road to the top of the mountain to the ancient Inca city. It was a wonderful sight. Seeing the ruins in the early morning mist as the sun rose over the peaks was amazing. It was mind-blowing to ponder how such a place had been built all those hundreds of years ago?

From Aquas-Calientes, or Machupicchu Pueblo as it's also known, it was a long bus ride to the city of Arequipa, which I recall was a lovely town with lots of flowers everywhere but I don't remember much else about it. Nor can I remember how long we stayed before we embarked on yet another overnight coach journey to Nazca. We arrived at Nazca at 3am where the owners of our hotel were not at all pleased to be woken by our taxi driver shouting loudly and banging on the front door of the hotel. Early the next morning we all squashed into a tiny aeroplane and flew over the desert to view the famous Nazca lines. They are quite incredible. Poor Cass had to struggle to keep her breakfast down although we had been advised not to eat before the flight.

Yet another long distant coach took us from Nazca to Paracas, a distance of some 300 miles along the Pan-American Highway. Paracas is a national park and is famous for the huge colonies of Elephant seals on the offshore islands. A not-too seaworthy boat took us out to see them as well as to watch the indigenous people harvesting guano from the cliffs. The guest house we had booked to stay in was awful so we moved to somewhere more salubrious. I foolishly deposited my wallet in the hotels safe at reception for safe keeping (there being none available in the rooms) only to find I had been robbed of $900 dollars when I retrieved it. The management of the hotel were astonished and bewildered that such a thing could happen of course.

The coach journey back to Cuzco took 9 and a half hours and was interminable. There were frequent stops along the way to stretch our legs and relieve ourselves but I thought it would never end. Refreshments were included in the price of the ticket and these turned out to be limp slices of bread with a mysterious filling and a bottle of Inca Kola. Inca Kola is a yellowish liquid and has an unusual taste, which I didn't much care for, but the local population love the stuff. Back at Cuzco we stayed in the same place as before and I enjoyed some more matte. On the final leg, we took a splendid train across the Alto Plano and down the famous scissors' switchbacks to Miraflores. Cass went back to Chile and we returned home after an exhausting but worthwhile adventure.

Australia

2005 saw Anna, Cass and I embark on a trip to Australia. We stopped off at Singapore; the Island City-State whose emblem is a Lion, for three days staying in the Traders Hotel at the quiet end of Orchard Road. James was back-packing in Oz at the time and we planned to meet up with him in Sydney. En-route to Sydney we stopped off at Melbourne to visit Anna's Uncle David Rennison and Aunty Teddy (Edwina I think). Uncle David is Peggy's younger brother. He and his family had emigrated to Australia in the 1950's availing of the £10 assisted passage scheme that was available at the time to encourage people to move to Australia. (Scornfully maligned by the Aussie's as 'Ten-Pound Poms'). Before Uncle David emigrated, he had owned a market garden business in North County Dublin and on arrival in Melbourne had found employment as a gardener at Government House (before the Capital was transferred to Canberra) ultimately attaining the position of head gardener upon retirement.

They now lived in a suburb of the city, named Mordialloc and we took a suburban train to visit him and his family; his sons Michael, and Nicholas and their families. David's daughter

Susan and her husband Pete live in New Zealand so we didn't get to meet them, but we did meet Mike and Nicky and their families. (I'm afraid I can't remember all their names). They were all very friendly and sociable and entertained us to a superb barbeque. Nick took us for a trip in the speed-boat he owned but unfortunately it broke down and left us stranded and adrift on the ocean till we were rescued. Sadly, it was the last time Anna saw Uncle David as he died a year later, so it was good that we had made the effort to visit.

From Melbourne we flew up to Sydney and met James and his old school friend Noel Warren. They had been working together driving huge combine harvesters on farms in the outback. James had booked us into the Rocks Hotel which was right on the harbour with views of the Bridge and the Opera House. We did a lot of sightseeing around the city; visited Luna Park and took a water taxi out to Bondi Beach. Later we hired a car and drove up into the Blue Mountains and stayed overnight in the Carrington Hotel, in Katoomba. An old-fashioned Western style hotel with bat-wing doors and balconies. Next day we drove to Jervis Bay, a place Cass wanted to see because it was where one of her favourite Aussie soap-operas, 'Home and Away' was filmed. At the end of the trip, it was a bit sad to say goodbye to James before the three of us returned to Ireland stopping in Singapore again. James eventually returned home the following year.

Far East

2006 we again headed East. The four us flew to Singapore for a few days arriving in time for New Year's celebrations where we partied at an open-air bar and enjoyed the fireworks. I was amazed at how much Singapore had changed since I was stationed there when serving in the Royal Navy during the 1960's. I hardly recognized anywhere. All the old haunts such as Albert Street, the China Fleet Club, Bogis Street and the Sembawang Naval Base had all been swept away and replaced with tower blocks and modern buildings. Fortunately, the fabulous Tiger Balm Gardens (also known as the Haw Par Villa Gardens) has survived. Singapore is a very clean city. I was most impressed by how well maintained the city is; I don't remember seeing a single piece of litter anywhere. In fact, during a boat trip on the Singapore river Anna made to throw her cigarette-end (yes, she was still smoking then) into the water when the boatmen stopped her, took a tin from his pocket and bade her to put it in. The zoological gardens on the Island are without doubt one of the best zoos I've ever seen. Singaporeans are very proud of their island city.

From Singapore we took a train to Kuala Lumpur. Not a very fast train with frequent stops, but the air-conditioning was super-efficient; it got so cold that we had to retrieve our fleeces from our suitcases to keep warm. In K.L. we had of course to ascend the dizzying height of the spectacular Petronas Towers. We flew from K.L. to Penang where I visited some of the old haunts from my Navy days. (Naval personnel on long tours were permitted to take leave there for R and R). We also saw the famous butterfly farm which housed some of the largest and most colourful insects I've ever seen.

A ferry took us from Penang to Langkawi which was a day's sailing. Anna and I stayed at the Bon Ton resort in a traditional Malay hut built on stilts. There was no air conditioning and we were eaten alive by mosquitoes. It was very basic accommodation; the shower drained straight through the floor to the outside for example, but it was interesting and different never-the-less. James and Cass stayed in a comfortable air-conditioned hotel. Langkawi is only a small island so we were able to see most of in a day in the car we hired. We stopped for lunch at the Four Seasons Hotel and admired the gold-plated fixtures in the loos.

Our final stop of the tour was Bangkok. A city that is the total opposite of Singapore; it is dirty, smelly and overcrowded, but even so: exciting. We visited the famous golden Buddha and toured the city in Tuk-tuks. (The curious three-wheel rickshaw motorbikes that are used as taxis). A visit to Patpong night market was a memorable experience.

Trying to pack too much into four weeks was a mistake; attempting to do too many things in too shorter time left us fatigued and drained and we were all glad to get back home.

Chang Mai

2007 took Anna and I to Thailand again to stay in The Ramada Hotel, in Chang Mai. Being 700 km further north, Chang Mai has a much cooler climate than Bangkok and was therefore far more pleasant, but the smog and air quality was very bad. We did the usual things including riding on an elephant in the sanctuary that has been established for sick and orphan pachyderms. I was slightly dismayed to see these noble beasts being made to play football and paint pictures.

Canada/US

During 2007 we also visited James in Vancouver where he was now living. When he first arrived there, on his way to the Far East he liked the place so much he decided to stay and not go on to Thailand as had been his original plan. Vancouver is a lovely city; clean and modern with many municipal parks, a brand-new metro system and efficient trolly buses.

In 2008 we visited Vancouver again and stayed with James.
Whilst there we took the opportunity to hop down to San Francisco for a week, another place on my bucket list I have always wanted to visit. James came with us but unfortunately our visit coincided with a massive convention of computer geeks which meant that all the best hotels had been booked and the one we ended up in, The San Remo Hotel wasn't great. But we did the usual

tourist stuff; we rode the cable cars, visited Alcatraz and Haight-Ashbury, took a boat trip to see the Golden Gate bridge and ate at Fisherman's Wharf.

Mexico/Cuba

2009 we flew to Cancun in Mexico via Atlanta, Georgia. We stayed in an all-inclusive resort named Playa del Carmen. We were accommodated in our own exclusive chalet together with a conscientious personal concierge to assist us with our every needs. It was most agreeable to lie by the pool and order Pina Coladas's from the ever-attentive waiters. Cass and Queno joined us from Chile and James came down from Vancouver. After our stay in Playa del Carmen, we rented a car and drove the 100 or so miles to stay in the Hacienda Xcanatun near the ancient capital of Merida. The hacienda had once been a huge farm that grew Agave the cactus used in the production of
Tequila and Mezcal. The place was so large it had its own railway network with an extensive system of tracks extending throughout the property. I was interested to see several rusting and abandoned

locomotives and rakes of trucks in sidings and sheds!

From there we visited the ancient Mayan temples at Chichen Itza and where I suffered a bout of sun-stroke requiring me to stay in a darkened room for 24 hours.

At the end of our stay in Mexico the others went their separate ways and Anna and I flew to Cuba, which is only a 30-minute flight from Cancun. Our hotel in Havana was the Hotel Manzana Kempinski La Habana, which overlooked one of the main squares. The city is still stuck in the 1950's and has many fine old buildings that are all in desperate need of repair and some TLC. They don't appear to have been touched since Castro's Communist revolution. When Fidel Castro kicked the Americans out, they left behind a whole lot of their cars that are still in use today. It was fascinating to see ancient Chevrolet's, Cadillac's and Pontiac's being driven around and used as taxis. We visited the former home of Ernest Hemmingway and saw the Nobel Prize he'd won for literature and the typewriter upon which he had written 'The Old Man and the Sea'.

France

Also, in 2009 Jonathon and Susan Bailey invited us together with a group of their friends to stay at a chateau in France owned by Susan's uncle or cousin. Named La Baurde it is in Provence near the city of Avignon. They kindly invited us to stay with them during the summers of 2010, 11,12 and 13. After a week or ten days with them we usually moved on for a stay at a holiday resort. That first year we went to Tossa del Mar on the Spanish Costa Brava. In the following years we visited Barcelona, Biarritz, Carcassonne and Avignon. During the summer months Eurostar ran a train service from St Pancras in London direct to Avignon via Paris which was very expedient. The journey didn't take much longer than it did to fly from Dublin to Exeter and then to Avignon, which was the normal route. To my mind the train was far more enjoyable and relaxing. (Anna didn't agree).

Chile/Argentina

In 2010 we visited Cass in Chile and during our stay Anna and I flew to Mendoza in Argentina for the weekend to see the city and take in a few wine tours. Mendoza is a well-known wine producing region which has many famous labels. At about 0330 on Saturday 27th February, we were awakened when our hotel bed began violently shaking. It was not until the next morning that we discovered that Chile had been hit by a magnitude 8.8 earthquake (or Terre moto in Spanish). As a result, the airport in Santiago had been badly damaged and closed meaning that we were unable to fly back, but we managed to secure tickets on a coach that brought us back over the Andes. This proved to be an interesting journey. It included a stop for customs at the border crossing between Argentina and Chile which is on the top of a mountain. When we alighted from the coach for a passport check we found to our dismay that the temperature was way below freezing with deep snow drifts all around. We'd left Mendoza dressed in shorts and tee-shirs not realizing that we would be crossing over 5000-meter peaks. It was very cold as the customs post was completely exposed to the elements. We were very glad to get back onboard the bus for the drive down the hundreds of hairpin bends onto the Chilean plain. (A drive almost as scary as Cuzco to Pisac).

Cass had been very frightened during the earthquake. Benjamin, their first child was still under a year old and of course was totally dependent. They were living at the time on the 27th floor of a high-rise apartment block in Providencia, and had to evacuate the building without the use of the elevators. Luckily there was very little damage to their flat - only a few cracked tiles in the bathroom. The building requirements in Chile are very strict and ensure that most newer building survive with minimal damage. We left Chile a few days later with aftershocks still being felt; one happened as we waited to board our flight to London which was very alarming. I was never so glad to get into the air.

While we were in Mendoza, we went to a restaurant for a meal in the evening and while sitting at our table who should we spot but Pat and Liz Faulkner, friends from Ireland. They happened to be touring South America and had arrived in Mendoza that day.

It was an extraordinary coincidence to meet people we knew, who just happened to be in the same restaurant at the same time as we were and in such a remote place What are the odds?

During this period, we had moved house again from Tristenagh in Glenbrien to Barntown into a bungalow named Derravaragh and it was while living here that we purchased a camper van. Initially we had planned to use it to tour the UK and even Europe but as it turned out we hardly used it at all. When we did have time off from work, we usually went abroad or visited Canada and Chile. So, it was only on Bank Holidays or the odd weekend that we got to use it, but we never-the-less still managed to see a lot of Ireland that we wouldn't have done otherwise.

France

In 2010 Cass and Queno came to Ireland. We loaned them our camper-van so that they could visit their friends in Ireland and the UK. Before they returned to Chile, we rented a house near Grasse in the South of France for a family holiday. We hired a large car and from the house we made daily trips to Nice, Cannes, and Monte

Carlo (where James and I walked the Monaco Grand Prix circuit). We drove up into the Alpes-Maritimes and saw the lavender fields that were in glorious bloom. James was mad into photography at the time so we had constantly to stop so that he could photograph them and whatever else caught his eye.

Canada

We had planned to spend Christmas of 2011 in Vancouver with James and Khudeja. The winter in Ireland that year was a very cold with a lot of snow and our original flight to Vancouver was cancelled due to the weather. Luckily, we managed to secure a flight after Christmas to Seattle. James and Khudeja drove down from Vancouver and we spent New Year's there staying in the Sheraton Hotel. We attended a New Year's Eve dinner and dance party in a different hotel and watched the fireworks display on the Space Needle. On top of all the delays and changes of plan the United Airline lost Anna's luggage. Happily, it was recovered before we left for Vancouver.

Anna's Journeys

During these years Anna also made several trips on her own. On one she took a group of visually impaired people to Thailand for two weeks trekking in the jungle and river rafting. I was amazed and impressed that she undertook such a venture and that NCBI financed it. She was also appointed as Irelands representative on some sort of International Technology committee for NCBI that involved annual conferences in among other places Thessalonica in Greece, Helsinki in Finland and Baku in Azerbaijan. In Azerbaijan she was treated with a great deal of suspicion being suspected of spying. She was several times interviewed by the political police much to her disquiet.

Malta

In 2012 we went to Malta and Gozo for a week after staying at La Baurde and it was in Malta that Anna slipped and fell by the hotel's rooftop swimming pool and broke her leg. It was set and plastered before we were invalided back to

Ireland via Frankfurt, Germany. Anna spent many weeks with her leg in a cast. She needed an operation to insert a steel rod and pins into her tibia and fibula both of which had been broken. At that time, we owned a Honda CRV which was a blessing because it was big enough to get Anna and her wheelchair in and out without too much difficulty. I believe that the subsequence re-appearance of the cancer (see the following section) in her bones was the result of this fracture.

Amsterdam

2013 was our last year of holidays. For my birthday in April, we made a weekend trip to Amsterdam to see among other things the newly reopened and re-furnished Rijks Museum where the famous painting 'The Night Watch' by Rembrandt hangs. We also took a train to Den Haag and saw the multi-coloured tulip fields. Unfortunately, Anna was in a lot pain from her leg and wasn't able to walk a great deal.

La Baurde/ Carcassonne

Later in the summer Anna insisted we accept Jonathon and Susan Bailey's invitation to La Baurde although she was finding it increasingly difficult to walk. On our way home we took a train from Avignon to Carcassonne but Anna was virtually confined to the hotel room because it was too painful for her to walk. I toured the towns famous Citadel alone. We flew back from Carcassonne to Dublin with Ryanair and I managed to arrange a wheelchair and assistance from the airline which helped. This was to be the last holiday we spent together for she died in the spring of the following year.

Chile

After Cass married Queno in 2005 and took up permanent residence in Chile, we visited them most years. We timed our visits to be at Christmas and New Year, mainly because it was lovely to spend Christmas with their growing family but also because it was summer in the Southern Hemisphere which meant we could escape an Irish winter. Over the years we took many trips from Santiago. We visited Buenos Aires, Rio de

Janeiro and Mendoza and had holidays at places in Chile such as La Serena, Pucon, Santa Cruz, Matazan, Vina del Mar and Valparaiso. The holidays in Chile were a great opportunity to see the country. Cass would usually rent a cabana or an apartment which was more convenient and less expensive with kids in tow. We several times visited Queno's parents Mirta and Raul Medina who lived in Rancagua.

Anna's Cancer Journal

In 2007 Anna discovered a lump in her breast. Her GP Dr Mary Maher sent her for a biopsy and it was found to be malignant. Dr Maher then referred her to an oncologist, Dr Paula Calvert at Waterford Regional Hospital and after consultations with a surgeon and a radiologist it was decided that an operation was necessary. A mastectomy was performed and her lymph glands were removed by Mr Tadros, a surgeon at Wexford General Hospital. Re-constructive surgery was carried out at the same time as the mastectomy. Unfortunately, the wound became seriously infected and the implant was removed. This infection, combined with a severe allergic reaction to a drug she'd been prescribed, caused her kidneys to fail. She was blue-lighted to the Beaumont Hospital in Dublin where she spent several days on dialysis. It was a tense week but thankfully she recovered.

When fully recovered from the kidney problem she began a course of chemotherapy in the Whitfield hospital in Waterford and a month or so after that was completed, she was admitted into St James Hospital in Dublin for six weeks of radiation therapy. About nine months after first discovering the lump she was declared free of cancer and remained so for the next 7 years.

In 2013 Anna began complaining of pain in her hip which she thought was a consequence of breaking her leg when we were on holiday in Malta. Her health began to decline after we returned from 'LaBaurde' in France earlier in the year where she'd been in serious pain. She continued to work although her heart wasn't in it; she had lost her enthusiasm for the job. She was prescribed progressively stronger pain killers. She visited osteopaths and sports injury specialists for massages and acupuncture, none of which helped much.

Over the months the pain became increasingly sever and I finally persuaded her to see Dr. Myles Deas who sent her for X-rays. (Dr. Maher had now retired). When these came back, they revealed dark spots on her pelvis and in the long bones in her legs. She saw Dr Calvert again in Waterford and it was decided that another course of chemo was necessary; a different regime from the breast cancer, a drug specifically targeting the bones.

As Anna health continued to fail, Dr Deas came out to the house to examine her as it was becoming increasingly difficult for her to travel. When he was leaving, I asked him for his opinion. 'She's dying' he said. I was truly shocked. Up until this moment I had firmly believed that she would eventually get well again. I had been in denial and now had to accept the reality.

As the disease got progressively worse Anna was less able to do things for herself and I was finding it harder to help her. Then one night she fell as she was getting out of bed to use the commode and I had great difficulty lifting her back into bed. I finally had to acknowledge that I needed some help. I called the palliative care nurses based in Wexford hospital and they came immediately and took charge. They arranged for various aids including a medical bed that cranked up and down, an orthopaedic armchair, a new commode and other gadgets to be supplied. They also arranged for a woman, Tess Morrisey to call every day to assist me with general help like bathing and changing her clothes.

When Anna became bedridden a night nurse was also arranged. The palliative care nurses called every day to check on her and organize whatever medication she required and call the CareDoc if he was needed. They also regularly turned her over, changed her catheter and administered the drugs she'd been prescribed.

Eventually she slipped into a coma and about a week later at 2:17 pm she passed peacefully away. During her final days we each took turns to sit with her as she lay unconscious and Liz was with her when she finally died. James, Cass and Khudeja were with her in the house at the time. Khuds had flown in from Canada two days earlier with her new born baby boy, Adam. He had been born four weeks premature and was barley three weeks old. He was the tiniest baby I've ever seen.

Macken's Funeral Home made all the necessary arrangements for the funeral such as the flowers, coffin, hearse and the grave digging. Their fees were paid for by The Credit Union with which we had an account.

The funeral service took place at St Iberius' Church in Wexford town and was conducted by Rev Maria Jansen. Anna was then interned in St Ibar's cemetery at Crosstown just across the river from the town. As is customary at Irish funerals 100's of people attended including all her many friends and work colleagues. Anna was well known in the town and the county because of her work with the blind and everyone who knew her came to pay their respects. After the burial drinks and refreshments were provided in the Riverbank Hotel.

Eulogy for Anna delivered by Rev Maria Jansen.
6th May 2014. St Iberius Church, Wexford.

On behalf of all of us gathered here in honour of Anna, may I extend our heartfelt sympathy to you Neil, James and Cass, to you Liz, to Khudeja and to all Anna's friends from far and near. We remember particularly her Benjamin and Matteo in Chile and baby Adam aged 6 weeks who came just before Anna died and to Queno, her son-in-law.

Anna was a Dublin woman who after college went to Stratford upon Avon with Liz for work and there met Neil whom she married on 29th June 1974 and they came to Ireland in 1975 to Wexford where Anna's father had bought a farm in Garryduff. Cass and James were reared in Wexford.

Last Sunday when taking a service in Tramore, a parishioner came up to me after the service, Christine Earl, deeply upset to read of Anna's death in the paper and she asked that I extend her deepest sympathy and that of her husband Dean David Earl to you, her family. Christine told me that at a very hard time in the parish of Ferns when parishes were being amalgamated into parochial unions, Anna as a young woman came forward and trained as a parochial reader and took services each Sunday. She was Dean Earl's right-hand person and did monumental work in that parish for nigh on ten years or so. They were so upset to hear of her death and I'm sure that is the case for many, many people.

I met Anna for the first time at the time of her mother's dying in Kerlougue Nursing Home. Her mother was just a lovely woman. Later I met her at events run by NCBI – one remarkable occasion when the South East branch members made and built a traditional Wexford Cut boat and launched it from Killurin. Both Anna and Liz worked in the NCBI at that stage and Anna was Liz's boss! To her team there she was mentor and rock and they are just bereft at her death. She had a genuine care for others, and an ability just to do the right thing when needed, to make that call, remember that sick relative… the list is endless. She was known for her accuracy of judgement and fair-minded ability to see issues from both sides Her wisdom was sought and valued.

Behind that immense commitment to her work and to the wellbeing of others, (she helped set up the Mrs Quinn charity shops, for example) family was hugely important. She insisted that Neil keep in touch with his family in England and they had planned to retire there in a year or two.

As Cass lives in Chile and James in Vancouver, it was a good job that she adored travelling. They always arranged to meet during holiday time and Anna always researched her holidays thoroughly – given that her degree was in geography. She was a voracious reader – and Kindle meant that she did not have to bring 20 books for a two-week holiday.

When we met on Friday, a few things became very clear as her family spoke of her. Anna was a profoundly good person, loved and loving, wise and independent, generous to a fault, one to whom one turned for advice, imaginative and utterly non-judgemental. Khudeja spoke with such affection for her mother -in-law – as wise and a superb listener.

Six years ago, Anna overcame breast cancer but two years ago she had a fall when on holiday – then bone cancer took its grip. Neil's care was total, utterly patient and utterly attentive to her needs. She did not speak of her feelings or fear. Even when she was in hospital, she was thinking of others. Some older people could not grasp the buzzer to get the nurses, so Anna got 'bump on's – little plink rubber buttons that made finding and using the buzzers easier. Her care for others was always imaginative – and practical.

Over the last weeks of her illness Neil said that the care of the Hospice Home Care Team and the Cancer Society night nurses made her last days much more comfortable. And he would like to thank particularly Nurse Liz McGarry and care assistant Tess Morrissey for their great help.

Over the years of her time as parish reader, Anna would have led worship diligently. Her humanity spoke volumes about the foundation of her life. – care- love, kindness. The epistle speaks that those who live in God are the ones who love. That is what the whole thing is about. All else is piffle. No one had ever seen God but if we love God, he is in us. Anna Williams' engagement with many, many lives was the touch of genuine goodness. Let us all learn from that and let that care be her greatest legacy.

Finally, and now I address the community here in Wexford – look after Neil, Liz, Cass and James who'll return to West Cork, Chile and Canada and to the house that will be dreadfully lonely. As she cared for you, please care for Neil because he gave his all to her when she needed it most.

Let our care for others be the way we pay respect to Anna Williams' life.

Amen.

Epilogue

Ireland changed enormously during the 40 years I lived there. In 1975 when I first arrived the country was still pretty much the equivalent of a third world country. The roads and infrastructure were appalling as were the Social Services. The country was held in the inflexible grip of the Catholic Church; nothing could be done or approved of without first gaining their consent. Joining the European Union and the scandals surrounding the clergy helped to bring about the country's transformation into the modern society it is today.

The revelations of the rampant child abuse within the catholic church, particularly of Father Brendan Smith and other priests hastened the decline in their power and respect. One such case happened in the nearby village of Monogear where the parish priest Father James Grennan was exposed as a paedophile. And when it was revealed that Bishop Eamon Casey of Galway had fathered a secret child with the American Annie Murphy the Catholic Church lost a lot of its credibility and deference.

During this 40-year period Ireland was visited by two US Presidents – Reagan and Clinton and a Pope – John Paul II. The nation elected two female presidents – Mary Robinson and Mary McAlesse. The Punt was abandoned in favour of the Euro when Ireland joined the European Monetary System. Homosexuality was decriminalized, divorce and same-sex marriages were legalized and the abortion laws were relaxed. And finally, the Good Friday agreement was signed on 10th April 1998 bringing an end to the many years of conflict in Northern Ireland.

On the 8th of February 1983 the Aga Khan's Derby winning racehorse *Shergar* was kidnapped by the IRA from his home at Ballymany Stud, Co. Kildare. A ransom of three million euros was demanded for his safe return. This was not paid and the horse was never seen again.

There were three major bank strikes during the sixties and seventies. (Curiously they all occurred during the summers). We were living in Ireland for the last one which lasted from June to September 1976. Surprisingly these closures didn't cause too much economic upheaval as Ireland survived on a cash society (known as the black economy) and a cheque system where cheques were repeatedly endorsed and passed from payee to payee. At the end of the strike, these cheques were all mostly honoured. Pubs and supermarkets largely took over the job of the clearing banks. Some estimates put the value at as mush as 3 billion punts in circulation between cash and cheque values.

The oil crisis of 1973 and 1979 forced bank interest rates up. At one point we were paying 25% on our farm loans. Not surprising then, that Ireland was known as 'the sick man of Europe' during that time.

Also, during these years Anna lost both her parents; her father from a heart attack (2001) and her mother from old age (2005). My mother passed away (2006). My father had died many years ago when I was only 18. Keith Edkins, my sister Jane's husband died in 2010. Liz Mellon (Anna's sister) married Fiona Reed in a civil ceremony in Dublin and they bought a house in Allihies in West Cork where they now live.

About ten years after we'd left Garryduff we went back for a visit and I found to my sorrow that the house had not been lived in since we'd departed. Gawping in through the dirty windows I could see that damp was beginning to affect the walls and the outside was becoming overgrown with weeds and bushes. Sadly, the new owners had also demolished the old coach house; a wonderful wooden structure that had survived from the previous century having been built in the 1880's. Also destroyed when the coach house was swept away were the colony of bees that had inhabited the space between the inner and outer walls of the building. They had lived there undisturbed for long before we came to Garryduff. Many of the beautiful old stone out-buildings had gone too, to be replaced with modern sheds. The new owners had also built a huge two-storied dwelling house; an ugly eye-sore, at the top of the lane beside the entrance gateway. It was so sad that the doors to Garryduff House had been locked and the house abandoned. The house that had given us so many years of happy memories and had been a major part of my family's life, was now deserted. They say that you should never go back to places you once lived in and I can see why.

Living in England is totally different from living in Ireland. The quiet clean country life had been replaced by the noisy polluted traffic-filled streets. The song of the skylark replaced by car horns.

Having lived in England for 7 years now I find I still very much miss Ireland. I miss the general friendliness of everyone. There would always be a cheery hello or a 'howya' whenever you met someone walking along the streets of Wexford town or Enniscorthy. People always had time to stop and talk. When driving around you'd always get a friendly wave from the other driver whether you knew the person or not. In contrast, when walking the crowded streets of Stratford, one rarely makes eye contact or nods or smile; peoples gazes are fixed on the ground or on their phones.

In Ireland the countryside was just outside the door of Garryduff. It was common to see foxes, badgers, stoat, weasels, hedgehogs and in one clean stream I was familiar with; otters. Birdsong was always audible. It was a common sight to see pheasants, magpies, rooks, crows, barn owls, and hawks. Although it was less common it was still possible to see kingfishers, jays, partridge, hooded crows, and even the odd corncrake. The Spring of every year would see the arrival of squadrons of swallows coming in from Africa to nest in the barns.

In contrast to this idyllic setting there are only a few country walks around Stratford; the 'Rec' or recreation meadow is one but it is always crowded with people, cars and bicycles. One popular walk is known as 'The Greenway', the defunct railway track from Stratford to Long Marston and Honeybourne but this is inevitably crowded with dog walkers, joggers and cyclists.

Lastly, anyone who loses a spouse or a partner will know what it is like to be suddenly alone. It is a unique experience; a major change to your world. All of a sudden not talking to someone you talked to every day leaves a huge hole. Not sharing a G&T at the end of the day and discussing the day's events, or relating a piece of gossip or an anecdote is big loss. The absence of those intimate moments and the empty bed are difficult to come to terms with. But as the years pass the loneliness gets easier to endure; you move on, the grieving becomes less, and you no longer think of her at every moment. However, there are still times when it will unexpectedly hit me that I'll never see my uxorious Anna again.

In Memory of Anna Williams nee Mellon
1950 – 2014
Rest in Peace

Scholars Court, Stratford upon Avon,
Warwickshire.
February 2021.

Author Bio.

Neil Williams moved from England to Co Wexford, Ireland in 1975 where he farmed and raised his family. He left Ireland in 2015 when his wife passed away and moved to Stratford upon Avon where he now spends his time travelling and visiting his grandchildren in Chile and Canada. This memoir is his debut as a chronicler

Printed in Great Britain
by Amazon

25053441R00076